"I have known James for 20 years and his pub stories are the stuff of legend...

...Dowdes is the pub expert. He's like Dr. Pub."

RUSSELL HOWARD

"My ideal pub is somewhere in the middle of nowhere. It has a roaring fire with a dog curled up nearby, plenty of decent ale, James Dowdeswell is sat at the bar, telling stories, and there is no bell for last orders."

JON RICHARDSON

The PUB Manifesto

A Comedian Stands Up For Pubs

JAMES DOWDESWELL

CAMRA BOOKS

Published by the Campaign for Real Ale Ltd
230 Hatfield Road
St Albans
Hertfordshire AL1 4LW
www.camra.org.uk/books

Design and layout © Campaign for Real Ale Ltd. 2018
Text © James Dowdeswell

First published 2018

ISBN 978-1-85249-355-4

A CIP catalogue record for this book is available from the British Library.

Printed and bound in the United Kingdom by Cambrian Printers Ltd.

Head of Publishing: Simon Hall
Project Editor: Katie Button
Editorial Assistance: Emma Haines
Sales & Marketing: Toby Langdon
Design/Typography: Dale Tomlinson

Photos: cover (front and back) Cath Harries; p. 2 Demetrius Deech;
p. 35 Phil Gammon; p. 53 Geoff Brandwood.

Contents

Preface: 'The Pub Kid' 6

1   The Sobering Pub Situation 9

2   Of Course the Romans Invented Pubs 19

3   George Orwell and the Genesis of The Pub Manifesto 37

4   Pub Location, Pub Location, Pub Location 47

5   Interior Design, Darling 57

6   Toilet Tales 65

7   Not Beer Gardens, but Biergärten 69

8   Beer, Both Real and Otherwise 75

9   Agricultural Champagne 93

10 All About Stout 105

11 A Sideways Glance at Wine in Pubs 117

12 Sheep Dip and Pig's Nose Whisky 129

13 Chin Chin for Gin 139

14 The Dreaded Top Shelf, behind the Bar 151

15 Soft Drinks and the Designated Driver 161

16 Beer Monster Munchies 169

17 Food, Glorious Food 175

18 Customer Service and the Art of Bartending 185

19 Let the Music Play (or not) 195

20 Pub Games and Entertainment 201

21 TV, Wi-Fi, Phones and Moans 213

22 Pub Dogs and Other Animals 221

23 Conclusion and the Sun Across Water 231

Bibliography and Further Reading 235
Acknowledgements 236

'The Pub Kid'

I WAS BORN AND BREWED in a pub.
My Mum hails from Wales, the beautifully named Merthyr Tydfil, and my Dad is from Manchester. They met halfway in Bristol, at a party. My Mum's friends said:

> "You'll be ok with Mike, he'll take you out for a lovely dinner, you'll have a great time and won't see him again."

Don't be fooled, my Dad was not a 'playa', it was just that he was always working at the pub and was lucky if he got one evening off a week, and even then he had to be back by 10.30pm to close up. On meeting my Mum, he was instantly smitten and proposed on their third date. He bent his knee outside The Granary, off Queen Square, a famous Bristolian pub. When she accepted, they popped back in for last orders. My Dad claimed it was all in the timing.

My Mum was a schoolteacher, but gave it up to help my Dad run the pub. She sacrificed teaching schoolchildren how to grow up, in order to pull pints for grown-ups who acted like kids.

The most commonly asked question when someone finds out you grew up in a pub is "Did you get free drinks?" Yes, but only draught-flow coke and lemonade. Everything else had to be accounted for. In a bid to stop my sister and I coating our teeth with sugar, my parents told us Coca-Cola was actually made from coal. Looking back on it, I'm surprised I didn't also think the coal bunker consisted of Cola Cubes.

I was four when I tasted my first drop of beer. It was an accident. I leaned over a bucket of Bass, lost my balance and fell in. It was a case of drink or swim, and I drank. Of course I did, it was in my genes, and all over my jeans. Being baptised by beer at four years old was quite a feat. It was almost a religious experience and maybe why I have worshipped ale ever since. My sister Talia and I became self-appointed cellar assistants. Our main job was to whine the word "Why?" at every juncture.

The pub has shaped parts of my personality. I am a heavy sleeper and find night noise soothing. My bedroom was situated above the raucous public bar. Occasionally I would pick out an intriguing snippet of conversation, a word, a phrase or a song lyric, and add it to my vocabulary. I remember this having a profound effect on me at school, where I was already known affectionately as 'the pub kid'.

In the early '80s it was the norm to do PE in our vest and pants, even if you hadn't forgotten your kit. Only I didn't wear vests. I wore shrunken down T-shirts from the breweries. My favourite was my Theakston's T-shirt, which had the slogan 'I've got that Old Peculier Feeling' emblazoned on the back. This amused my teachers. I imagine, when we played dead lions, I must have looked like an abandoned beer mat, or the dying embers of a stag party.

Once, we had to sing a song in class. The first kid sang 'Baa Baa Black Sheep'. The second plumped for 'Little Miss Muffet'. I stood up gingerly and said:

> "I don't know the name of my song, but I heard it in bed last night."
> "Ok. Take it away James," encouraged the teacher.
> "Star of the Eaaassst, shining on the shit house door!"
> "Who taught you that?"
> "The rugby team miss."

I never got to finish my song in front of the class, but had to hum it silently on the naughty step.

The biggest event of my week was the arrival of thoe delivery trucks. When a truck pulled up, my parents would holler, "James, come quick, Mr Bass is here." We had given all the lorries names, as if in a boozy version of *Thomas the Tank Engine*.

I mean, why be a train spotter when you can be a beer spotter? There was Mr Bass, Mr Courage, and Mr Schweppes. Mr Bass was my favourite. It was the revered beer of the time, but I just liked the colours.

My parents' pub is perched on the banks of the River Severn. One morning my Mum woke us extra early, and explained that the pub downstairs had been flooded and we had to be rescued by the coastguards. Wow! What a start to the morning. I jumped out of bed and rushed halfway downstairs, only to be met by two coastguards. We were asked to jump into one of the coastguard's arms. My Mum probably didn't need to, but did anyway. Why not? Coastguards are like the firemen of the sea, aquatic sex gods. From there our family were ferried onto a motorised dinghy. It was quite surreal, jetting across the pub car park. Cars were bobbing in the water, and my Dad's old Triumph lurked just beneath the dirty floodwater, like a patient crocodile.

We were met on the banks of the floodplain by a police van, which escorted us to the local police station, where we given sugary tea and a biscuit. More *Heartbeat* than *Starsky and Hutch*, was the note in my diary. My parents' business was in ruins and the mood was sombre. I was sad too, because at one point I'd overheard someone say we might be rescued by helicopter. Hopping into a dinghy isn't quite as exciting as jumping into a chopper. That's why Arnold Schwarzenegger's characters never emerged from an Uzi firefight shouting, "Get to the dinghy!"

While the pub was being repaired, we decamped to one of my parents' friends. They managed a branch of Victoria Wine and lived in a flat above the premises. We had relocated from above a pub to above an off-licence. It seemed our family was destined to remain above booze.

The Anchor survived. Over the years my parents managed to adapt the pub without losing its history and atmosphere. This fluidity only extends to my Dad's business ventures; he still sports the same hairstyle and glasses. Ironically, very similar to the hair and glasses I now sport.

THE SOBERING PUB SITUATION

1

A S I TYPED THE chapter heading into my phone, the predictive text setting kicked in and suggested 'The So Wrong Pub Situation.' Maybe my phone was right.

We are in a catastrophic crisis. Eighteen pubs close per week in the UK. Eighteen! That is a shocking statistic. The tabloids constantly berate us for binge drinking and yet pubs are still going out of business. It doesn't make any sense. City analysts predict that, with this radical rate of decline, pubs may be extinct by the 2040s. This is unthinkable and not far off. So what can be done to save our beloved British boozer?

Pubs are community hubs. They are one of the cornerstones of British society and cannot be allowed to be called time upon. They are an idyllic institution, a one-stop shop for a plethora of purposes and possibilities. Where else can you celebrate, commiserate, socialise, hide, flirt, laugh, gossip, relax and let off steam, all at the same time?

There is something quintessentially British about pubs. The rest of the world languishes in bars, whereas the British pub is a proactive beast. We have to engage. Passivity is not an option. We approach the bar, jostle for position, scan the pumps and shelves for the drink of our choice, interact with the bar staff and acknowledge our fellow drinkers around us. Finally we emerge victorious, with not only our own drink paid for, but our friends' drinks as well. Compare this to a continental bar, where you secure a table, scour a menu and order from waiting staff who bring drinks from afar. It is a passive, disengaged experience and, at the end of the evening, you normally have to wait for an eternity for the bill to arrive and another eon for it to be processed. Imagine the frustrations of trying to embark on a continental bar crawl.

Some of the best nights of my life have been spent in pubs: turning 18, falling 40 and getting engaged. Perhaps the most magical nights of all are the spur of the moment, mid-week evenings, where you only pop out for the one drink, bump into friends and the night escalates beyond your wildest expectations. Pubs are more than just a meeting place; they're a refuge in which to regale stories, laugh, cry, sup and sing.

The pub is a great leveller, a rare place where everyone is equal. You can be a traffic warden or a high court judge, but in the pub there is no preferential treatment. We drink from the same glasses and sit on the same stools and sofas. It is a sanctuary, a home away from home.

A hundred years ago there was a huge gap between the living conditions of the rich and the poor. Those less well-off lived in small houses, the conditions were cold, damp, and dark, so people congregated in pubs for warmth, light and company. Some people are currently very well-off, and able to hang out at home and have dinner parties. But the reality for many of us, especially in big cities, is that we are living in shared housing, small flats or Harry Potter-style cupboards. We need the pub for our breathing and meeting space. We have gone full circle, and yet again the pub has become our front room.

The times they are a changing, and pubs need to evolve. Notorious train robber, Ronnie Biggs, returned to the UK aged 71 after hiding out in Brazil because he wanted to, in his words, "walk into a Margate pub as an Englishman and buy a pint of bitter." I would imagine he would have been shocked and confused at the current state of the English pub:

> *"What the hell is Curry Club; some sort of gang? Cream flow? If I wanted to get clotted, I'd have a Devonshire Tea. I fancy a fag. What do you mean outside? You starting summat?"*

You think Biggs might have been confounded. I have a nightmare vision of the pub 10 years from now. The happy hour will be unhappy, with bargain-basement £5 a pint deals. Bar staff will be history and replaced by a supermarket-style self-scan bar, with an annoyingly smug, robotic voice:

> *"Unexpected item in the drinking area. Did you bring your own recycled pint glass? Click here to redeem booze points."*

If that's not enough to make you flail your fists, an advert flashes up on a screen:

> *"Feeling sporty? Why not hire these infrared surround-sound wrap-around goggles where you watch your chosen sport from inside the ball."*

You spot another drinker, who is also gawping into his goggles, in between glugs of virtual beer. Of course, if you want to actually interact with fellow drinkers, you have to log on to the latest pub chat app, 'Banter', and if there were any bartenders to flirt with, you might click on 'Bar Tinder'.

The modern pub is up against it and faces competition from cheap supermarket booze, the smoking ban, coffee shops, not to mention TV, computer games, and box sets. Due to a spike in technology, we are now able to stream a myriad of TV shows and films from various devices at the click of a button. The rise of social media means people are now able to chat online or glean gossip from Facebook and Twitter rather than popping down the pub to find out the latest tittle-tattle.

Ten years ago, my friends and I would hit the pub every night. Now, with austerity biting and pints of beer where I live, in London, often hitting the £5 mark, it's cheaper and easier for my fiancée and I to have a drink in the comfort of our own home. When we do go out we don't always go to the pub, we might pop round to a friend's house, with a few cans or a bottle of wine. A visit to the pub is now a treat, rather than the main focus of our social lives. As a society, our drinking habits and priorities have changed, so how can the pub evolve with them?

One of the biggest impacts on pub trade is the appearance of inexpensive alcohol for sale in the supermarket. You can now buy a pint of beer for one-fifth the price you might pay in a pub. With the recession still biting, pubs are affected by simple economics.

Competition from the Supermarkets

Most supermarkets make very little profit on alcohol, but they use cheap booze deals to lure us in. However, do be aware that some booze deals are not as good as they seem. You often see wine bottles discounted at half price, but the discounted price point is actually what the wine is really worth. How do they do it? Simple. They double the price of the wine in one store, enabling them to declare it half price in another. This is all perfectly legal, but impishly sneaky.

The wide selection of affordable wine in the supermarket means most folk have a stash of wine at home, and may open a bottle when they come from work. My Dad claims "the ritual pouring of a glass of wine at 6 o'clock very often prevents them from driving to the pub that evening."

The Smoking Ban

The smoking ban was launched in July 2007. It changed pubs forever. We don't reek of smoke any more, but the lack of cigarette smoke has unmasked some previously unknown and unwelcome odours.

Before the ban, you flung open the door to a pub, on a cold night, to be greeted by a blast of warm air and a thick fug of dense smoke. It would take a few seconds for your eyes to adjust and pick out your friends, a spare seat, or sometimes even the bar. The billows of smoke, although poisonous, did lend a jazz-club atmosphere to the most banal of bars. However, when you got home, you had to jet wash all your clothes and hose down your hair. I'm surprised no one marketed a post-pub shampoo; Vidal Saloon, smoke and glow. Also, it was hard to deny you'd been to the pub when you smell like you've wrestled an ashtray. For people born after the late 1980s, who haven't experienced a smoke-infested pub, check out the smoking room in an airport. It looks like a chemistry test tube, mid-experiment.

E-cigarettes have recently become popular. Some people make them look cool, but I know I'd look like a Doctor Who fan, sucking on a sonic screwdriver.

I don't smoke but my mates do. When we go to the pub, they chat and flirt over a fag outside, while I'm stuck inside on my own, guarding the coats and bags. These days, it can seem as though it's non-smoking that's the anti-social behaviour.

Alcohol Units

One of the reasons the smoking ban came into force was that people became more health conscious in the noughties. It is widely known that the recommended medical amount of alcohol units per week were 21 for men and 14 for women. The problem is many of us rack up those units on a quiet night. The question is, where do those figures come from? Well, they were devised by the Royal College of Physicians in 1987. A panel was summoned by the government to make a recommendation on the amounts of units we may consume without causing health risks. According to Richard Smith, from the *British Medical Journal*, 'those (alcohol) limits were really plucked out of the air. They weren't based on any firm evidence at all. It was a sort of intelligent guess by a committee.'

WOW! So the scientific evidence to curb our drinking is actually guesswork. What's next? We only require four portions of fruit and vegetables per day? Incidentally, why are girls meant to drink less? The next time a doctor asks for your alcohol units per week, say 30. When questioned, state it was just an intelligent guess by a committee.

In 1995, the Department of Health switched their focus from our weekly intake to our daily alcohol units. They recommended imbibing no more than 3–4 units per day for men, and 2–3 for women. This equated to 28 and 21 units respectively. This transition from weekly to daily guidelines effectively increased our alcohol intake, for men by 33% and women, by a whopping 50%. However, the Department did warn the public that units should be spread over the week, rather than saving them up, like coupons, for one big session. They also added that everyone should have two to three alcohol-free days, which potentially meant two to three pub-free days.

In January 2016 the Department of Health amended their alcohol guidelines again, with alcohol being a proven link to cancer and heart disease. This time they advocated both men and women drink no more than 14 units of alcohol, to keep the health risks low. At least there was now equality between the sexes. This legislation equated to six pints of average-strength beer or seven glasses of wine a week. A good slogan might have been 'No more than a pint a day, keeps the doctor away.'

The Chief Medical Officer warned against binge drinking or, as he called it, 'Single-occasion drinking.' Would those folk who enjoy single-occasion drinking be henceforth known as S.o.d.s?

Not only have the government questioned our alcohol intake, it has also become commonplace to abstain from alcohol for two months of the year, with the rise of Dry January and Sober October. No wonder Halloween has become a bigger party in recent years. While these health initiatives are admirable, they do affect pub trade.

The Pubco Problem

OK, so the smoking ban, cheap supermarket booze, social media and health concerns are well documented. However, there is a fifth problem: pub companies. Pub companies, or pubcos as they are known, own huge portfolios of British pubs, and rent them out to tenants. This relationship is known as a pub tie. Enterprise Inns describe themselves thus:

> *'We are the largest pub company in the UK, with over 4,500 properties that are predominantly run as leased and tenanted pubs. We aim to partner with entrepreneurs passionate about pubs, by granting leases and tenancies to the best publicans.'*

Mitchells & Butlers currently own 1,700 pubs and restaurants, and Punch Taverns have 1,300 pubs. Unfortunately, some charge high rents, making it extremely tough for publicans to scratch a living. They also forbid landlords from choosing which products to stock. The tenants are 'tied' to the pubco, and have to buy their beer from the pubco's list. That is why you see handpump signs with 'Guest Beer' on tap, because that is the only beer the landlords can choose themselves. How frustrating. Surely one of the best things about running a pub is being able to choose what you sell and what tastes you represent.

After years of campaigning against the injustices of the tied house system, the Pub Code was introduced in July 2016, to try to create a fairer working relationship between the pubco and the tied tenant. According to Roger Protz, editor of the *Good Beer Guide*:

'At the heart of the code was the Market Rent Only (MRO) option. MRO will allow tenants to negotiate a contract with their pubcos, which will allow them to become 'free of tie' and able to buy beer and other products on the open market, paying their pubcos only market rents.'

The next stage is trying to enforce this code, and to help tied tenants with their negotiations.

It all began when the big pub companies borrowed heavily to create huge empires, in the 1980s. However, the financial crash of 2008 meant profits came tumbling down; debts needed paying, so they sold off their less successful pubs. CAMRA (the Campaign for Real Ale) estimated in 2008 that a third of these pubs were converted into flats, a third into cafés and restaurants, and the final third were demolished.

There are also independent property parasites – sorry, magnates (always get those two mixed up) – who buy up pubs as an investment and turn them into flats. The problem is, they believe the land a pub is built on is worth more than the pub itself. So what could be a lovely pub garden one day, could be a supermarket car park the next. Still, doesn't stop me drinking there though.

Tom Lamont wrote a brilliant investigative piece in *The Guardian* entitled 'The Death and Life of the Great British Pub' in which he stated: 'As a pub, the Parr's Head was worth roughly £500,000. With approval for it to be de-pubbed, the building was sold on for £1.3m. As six separate flats, it ended up going for a total just shy of £3m.'

The phrase 'de-pubbed' is an ugly one. Sounds like an unwelcome operation, and be careful with the number of Bs.

We want our pubs unique, sociable, welcoming, and brimming with personality. Not blemished by the corporate chains, forcing small independents out of business, and blotting the landscape of so many English towns. Years ago, British towns had history, culture and personality. These days all the high streets look the same. If you parachuted into the average town centre, you would be hard pressed to recognise which town you were in. Let's prevent pubs from falling into this bland, black hole.

Christopher Hutt wrote a book entitled *The Death of the English Pub*, back in 1973, which demonstrates that pubs have been in this position before, and recovered. The British pub has survived two world wars and the temperance movement. I am confident it can continue to prosper, despite its current obstacles. It's not all doom and gloom. We can all help, merely by choosing to drink in our local pub. Let's face it, as good causes go, it's one that keeps on giving.

OF COURSE THE ROMANS INVENTED PUBS

2

BEFORE WE can discuss the present and future situation of British pubs, we must first understand the past.

Monty Python fans will know that, of course, the Romans invented pubs. The Romans invented most good things, apart from the Roman sandal, which are nothing more than Latin crocs.

Two core skills the Romans brought to Britain were road building and brewing beer. Roadside taverns were built alongside Roman roads, where ale was brewed and sold. These pubs were called *Tabernae*, from which the word tavern derived. Besides wine, Roman soldiers also enjoyed a hard earned ale:

> *"Two goblets of Old Centurion and one Ides please. Et tu Brute?"*
> *"Beware The Ides of March Julius. Terrible drop.*
> *Gives you a dickie tummy. Are you aware of the new sewers?"*
> *"No."*
> *"You will be."*

Pubs have been central to British life since Roman times. They are part of our very DNA and need to be cherished and protected.

Ted Bruning, author of *Merrie England: The Medieval Roots of the Great British Pub*, recently asserted that the pub was invented by the French. After the invasion in 1066, he claims the Normans set up the first pubs, which were watering holes on the banks of the Thames, selling wine to visiting merchants. However, the notion that the British pub started as a French wine bar in Central London could seem to some as being positively medieval.

According to *Guinness World Records* the oldest pub is adjudged to be Ye Olde Fighting Cocks in St Albans. Documental evidence claims the pub traded from AD795. However other historians allege that the pub only arrived on its current site in AD1485. One other historic pub, Ye Olde Trip To Jerusalem, dates itself at AD1189. Nestled among the ramparts of Nottingham castle, it has a huge inscription on its white walls claiming to be 'The Oldest Inn In England.' But who is Ye Oldest? The plot thickens.

Pubs were often named after historical events. The Royal Oak was dubbed as a popular pub name after the tale of Charles II hiding in a hollow tree, after the battle of Worcester in 1651. These days the Royals have to escape from the paparazzi, but alas we may never drink in the Royal Tinted Limo, The Prince's Helicopter Pad or Uber HRH.

Originally pubs signs were just symbols with no text, as many people were illiterate. So a pub sign would just be a picture depicting a red lion, a swan or a wheatsheaf, for example. We have now gone full circle, with the youth of today embracing the use of emojis. What would a red lion with a thirsty face look like, I wonder?

In the Middle Ages everyone in Britain drank ale. As you may know, it was safer and more fun than water. Wine was too expensive and tea didn't become popular until the mid-17th century. So just imagine how much ale medieval builders consumed during an average work day:

"Would you tradesmen care for a beverage?"
"Absolutely, I would not dream of operating a piece of heavy machinery without at least a few pints inside me."

Monasteries brewed a bombastic amount of beer. In 1004 the average beer allowance for a monk in Burton Abbey was two gallons a day. That's 16 pints. SIXTEEN PINTS! I'd have a religious experience after that. In their defence, it's a lot easier to take a vow of silence when you're too drunk to speak.

Despite their own chastity, monks brewed beer to celebrate marriage. They called it Bride Ale, which is where the word bridal comes from. When I was a kid I spelt the word as bridle – maybe I liked horsey women.

Before the invention of drinking glasses, people drank from pig skins, pitchers, horns and bowls. As they were communal, your level was marked by a peg. Drinking more than your fair share became known as 'taking someone down a peg or two.' So presumably the aggressive stance of 'Oi! Did you touch my pint?' was originally 'Good sir, did you move my peg?'

Pubs were more than just a meeting place; for many folk they were the only place that was warm and dry. Beer would typically be served by the quart, which is a two-pint pot, so if the roaring fire didn't lift your spirits, the ale soon would.

Alehouses and Inns

In the middle ages there were two pub variations; alehouses and inns. Alehouses were actually people's houses. They brewed beer out the back and served it in the parlour. Most of the ale brewed in alehouses was produced and served by women, known as brewsters; they were the original home brewers. Everyone flocked to the house of the brewster who produced the best beer, which is where the term public house came from. Inns, on the other hand, were more of a commercial venture. They sold beer, wine and spirits, all of which was bought in, and they also provided food and lodgings.

The improved roads heralded the rise of the stagecoach and coaching inns. These beautiful buildings, with their spacious courtyards, catered for travellers, folks on pilgrimage and dandy highwaymen. They were the hotels of the day. Dick Turpin was the face of Ye Olde Premier Inn long before Sir Lenny Henry. In fact, in my opinion, more London pubs claim a connection to Dick Turpin than Edinburgh cafés to J K Rowling. But only just.

A great example of a coaching inn is the Grade I listed George Inn on Borough High Street, just down from London Bridge station, in Central London. Its historic courtyard has now become a delightfully cobbled beer garden, where I have sat many a time as a weary traveller, albeit as part of a pub crawl.

The George in Stamford, just off the Great North Road, is believed to have sheltered weary travellers for around 1,000 years. Unlike most inns, The George stretches across both sides of the road and has a gallows sign which unites the two. This ghoulish sign was installed to ward off highwaymen, and far more exciting than a motorway bridge linking two serving service stations. According to The George's website: 'No fewer than 40 coaches, twenty up and twenty down, passed through Stamford every day.' This refers to the direction the stage-coaches were travelling.

Gin

Adding to alehouses and inns, gin shops emerged in the late-17th century. In 1690 it was decreed that anyone could distil gin, if it was from English grain. That year the government also doubled the duty on beer. Britain went gin crackers. 'Drunk for a penny, dead drunk for tuppence' was the slogan of the day. No grey area there.

There was no stigma about drunkenness back in the 17th century. If you were too drunk, you were simply put in the stocks, whereupon judgemental citizens hurled rotten vegetables at your visage. Still, it sobered you up and was part of your five-a-day. We should bring back the stocks! It would be the perfect punishment for some. I am sure we can all think of a few malevolent figures in the public eye who it might be quite satisfying to fling a rotten cabbage at.

By 1740 gin was the drink of choice for the poor and half of the 15,000 drinking dens in London were gin shops. The UK was drinking six times more gin than beer. The effects were illustrated in two of William Hogarth's most famous illustrations, 'Beer Street' and 'Gin Lane'. Hogarth portrayed 'Beer Street' as distinguished and refined, whereas 'Gin Lane' was depicted as debauched and depraved. Public drunkenness was becoming a huge problem, so the ruling classes decided to push beer; after all, it was considered harmless.

The 1830 Beerhouse Act was a huge turning point in the development of pubs. Beerhouses were pubs that sold beer and cider, but not wines or spirits. The act was engineered to promote the healthy sustenance of beer, over the much-maligned gin. It allowed any beerhouse to sell beer and cider as long as they purchased a two-guinea licence. This resulted in a boom of beerhouses: '33,000 in the next two years', according to Geoff Brandwood, author of *Britain's Best Real Heritage Pubs*. The government was happy too, as it gained a new source of taxable revenue.

Over time gin shops developed into pubs. Their unique decadent style of mahogany bars, with ornate brass counters and mirrors, were all absorbed into the Victorian pub style we know and love today. Great examples include The Salisbury in St Martin's Lane in London, where I love to take my parents, and The Philharmonic Dining Rooms in Liverpool.

The Industrial Revolution led to steam trains replacing the stage coach, so pubs popped up next to train stations instead of just alongside major roads – although I'm sure a few rail replacement stage coaches appeared on Sundays.

By the end of the 19th century the pub landscape changed again as the bigger brewers, especially those companies who had floated on the stock exchange, began to snap up pubs like little green houses on a Monopoly board. They realised that, by owning a vast swathe of pubs, they could brand them with their own beers and build an empire. This was the start of tied housing.

The Temperance Movement

There was a Victorian backlash against alcohol at the turn of the century, with the rise of the temperance movement. It heralded from the United States, arrived in Britain in 1829, and by 1889 had secured a two million-strong support. The US yielded to the pressures of the movement and a country-wide prohibition on alcohol remained in place for 13 long years, from 1920 to 1933. Britain, however, refused to have the glass prised from its stiff upper lip, and alcohol flowed freely on this sceptred isle.

Here is a surprising fact for you: the football league was established in 1888 by the temperance movement as a way of keeping people out of the pub on a Saturday afternoon; well, that backfired! Indeed, it could be said to be the first own goal ever recorded.

According to George Ford, in his detailed historical account, *Thornbury Pubs*, by 1880 '43% of government revenue came from drink.' So the temperance movement, although worthy in some Puritan's eyes, severely threatened the country's potential taxable income.

David Lloyd George, the British prime minister in World War I, was a temperance supporter and was quoted as saying:

> *"We are fighting Germany, Austria and drink;*
> *and as far as I can see, the deadliest of those foes is drink."*

It sounds preposterous now. Reading that quote aloud, I couldn't help but recall the voice of General Melchett, Stephen Fry's character from *Blackadder Goes Forth*, complete with "Mwah!" at the end. Blackadder's riposte might be:

> "Indeed sir, and the best way to tackle an enemy is to befriend it first. Baldrick, fetch another few bottles of Bollinger from Darling's supplies. Let's see what we're dealing with."

In 1914 the government passed The Intoxicating Liquor Act. It wasn't intoxicating at all; if anything, quite the opposite. The word intoxicating is cold and anodyne. How can such a fun-less word be used to describe such a fun, fool-some act like drunkenness?

The Act limited pubs to opening five and a half hours per day (noon until 2.30pm and 6.30 until 9.30pm). This made being a publican a part-time job and freed up time for drinking – oh no, bar closed. These measures must have felt severe, as previously pubs opened as early as 5am. Nothing like a breakfast beer to warm the cockles if you can't sleep. More seriously, the Act also ordered beer to be watered down, and made it illegal to buy a round, as it might cajole others to drink at a faster rate.

Other clauses in the Act forbad the purchase of binoculars, writing in invisible ink abroad and feeding bread to horses. Rather than the tell-tale signs of being a spy, they sound like the hobbies of the Famous Five stranded in the country for their summer holidays. Also, who feeds bread to horses?

Despite these draconian cutbacks the plucky Brits drank more in the first six months of the war than in the whole of the previous year. Ironically, this benefitted the government, as the taxation incurred funded the war effort.

Inter-War Pubs

Predictably, rebuilding was the order of the day during the inter-war years. Housing estates emerged in an attempt to to provide an improved standard of housing. These new communities all had thirsts that needed quenching.

There was a race amongst the big brewers to build the biggest and best suburban pubs. But some felt these grandstanding pubs were nothing more than corporate carbuncles that ripped out the soul of the traditional pub and ostracised the common man. George Orwell wrote in his book *The Road To Wigan Pier*, first published in 1937:

> *'As for pubs, they are banished from the housing estates almost completely, and the few that remain are dismal sham-Tudor places fitted out by the big brewery places and very expensive.'*

Post-War Pubs

During the World War II pubs were seen as helping with the war effort. Of course they were, Churchill was in charge! He had his own Blitz spirit and was not afraid to drink it. He was the absolute antithesis of teetotal Lloyd George. In one of his speeches Churchill declared:

> *"Remember gentlemen it's not just France we're fighting for, it's champagne."*

As rousing sentiments go, for me, that is right up there with "Fight them on the beaches." I can imagine his generals clinking glasses and clucking accordingly. In fact, during the war the pub became less of a male domain and women started drinking in pubs.

After the war there was scarcely any money to rebuild pubs in their former glory, so prefabs sprouted up. These temporary huts could be constructed for a 10th of the cost of a traditional building. New towns like Stevenage and Kidderminster were emerging and they all needed new pubs. Britain was a phoenix rising from the post war ashes and people were philosophising, and reshaping their futures. Where better to do this than the pub? This was the idealistic backdrop from which George Orwell wrote an essay in the

Evening Standard, on 9 February 1946, in which he outlined his perfect pub. It was called 'The Moon Under Water.' He listed all his favourite attributes, before admitting it didn't actually exist; it was merely a fantasy. More on this in the next chapter.

The post-war years heralded a few key inventions, which became obstacles for the pub trade. The first espresso machine landed in 1952 and coffee bars were soon all the rage. Two years later the first Wimpy Bar sprouted in 1954. Would English pubs survive the American cultural overhaul? To paraphrase T. S. Eliot:

'Is this the way the pub ends, not with a bang,
but with a Wimpy?'

Watney's (a huge brewer and owner of a chain of pubs) saw the winds of change and even tried to put a Wimpy's burger counter in a pub. This was considered a maverick move at the time – no one went to a pub to eat. To contextualise, the first UK McDonalds did not open until 20 years later, in November 1974. The site was Woolwich in South-East London. These days, of course, burgers are staple pub grub.

Formation of CAMRA

By the late '60s a few large brewers, known as the Big Six, dominated the beer market. They each owned an empire of pubs, into which they pushed their own mass market, flavourless, keg beer. There was no variety and the beer was bland. Four men decided it was time for a taste intervention. So on Tuesday 16 March 1971, a date akin to the Battle of Waterloo for real ale enthusiasts, Michael Hardman, Graham Lees, Jim Makin and Bill Mellor founded the Campaign for the Revitalisation of Ale. According to CAMRA, these men formulated their campaign 'In the Westernmost pub in Europe – along the Kerry coast.' That description makes it sound like a secret Cold War treaty, plotted under the radar.

What also tickles me is that I doubt there was much real ale on offer in that remote Irish pub. Were the seeds of CAMRA really toasted with Guinness? If so, pure genius.

Once formed, CAMRA hit the ground running. At the AGM in 1973 CAMRA changed its name, although the acronym remained the same. They launched the now famous Campaign for Real Ale and announced they had secured 5,000 members. In 1974 the first *Good Beer Guide* was published and their headquarters set up in St Albans. In 1976 CAMRA became a limited company. But despite doing well financially they remained a charity organisation. In 1979, as the Conservatives marched into government, CAMRA set up the first Pub Preservation Group to oppose Pubcos and create a life raft for struggling pubs. In the first eight years of its existence, CAMRA put in place all the ideals it still holds dear today, championing fine real ale and real cider, while raising the pub's profile and protecting its interests. Total membership now resides at a whopping 183,000 and rising.

Theme Pubs

The first theme pub was introduced in October 1951 by Whitbread. It was The Nag's Head in Covent Garden, and they sensibly plumped for a theatrical theme. Photos of actors and actresses adorning the walls was said to give the pub a bit of West-End glamour, and it became a popular haunt for performers. Interestingly, keeping the name The Nag's Head, rather than plumping for a more theatrical name, gave the pub a subtler makeover. It was a great success and Whitbread launched a few more theme pubs, pairing pub paraphernalia with their surrounding interests. So the Coach and Eight in Putney commemorated the Oxford and Cambridge boat race, The Yorker in Piccadilly embraced cricket and The Railway Tavern in Liverpool Street was a trainspotter's delight. The themes seemed to be following a pattern of middle-class hobbies. How long before pubs emerged with names like The Stamp Collector's Tongue, and Chess Gang and Firkin?

The first Irish theme pub was arguably Flanagan's Apple in Liverpool, which opened in the mid-'80s. The founder, Bob Burns, was inspired by Irish pubs in New York, hence the name Apple. It was also situated in the Beatles Quarter of Liverpool, but the reference to the their record label, Apple, was probably a coincidence. There is a huge Irish population in Liverpool, who warmed to the theme of a New York-style Irish pub for people with Irish connections. Mulligan's in Cork Street, Mayfair, which opened in 1991, also lays claim to be the original Irish theme pub.

In the early 1990s Irish pubs were very popular. They were a fun, exotic place to be, everyone was welcome, all uniting under the idea of the craic. The social scene in the '90s was typified by lad and ladette culture, Blur versus Oasis, Euro '96 and nights out down the pub. It was all about having a laugh and not taking life too seriously. The Irish theme pub embraced drinking, singing and having the craic. It became big business and all the big breweries jumped on the bandwagon and built their own chain of Irish pubs; three of the best known were O'Neills (started by Bass and now owned by Mitchells & Butler), Scruffy Murphy's (run by Allied-Domecq) and Finnegan's Wake (owned by Scottish & Newcastle). By the late-'90s the Irish theme pubs' popularity waned. Tellingly, Flanagan's Apple doesn't even refer to itself as an Irish pub on its website any more.

Similarly, Walkabout sold a slice of the Aussie lifestyle to the UK with their Australian themed pubs. They began with the Outback bar in Covent Garden in 1995, under the umbrella company Walkabout. When the bar was so successful they decided to expand, they did so under the Walkabout name.

Wetherspoon's

Wetherspoon's emerged as super pub in the mid-'90s and spawned a succession of imitation pub chains. Like all success stories though, it didn't happen overnight. Tim Martin, the founder, liked his local pub so much that he bought the lease in 1979. It was originally called Martin's Free House, but was rebranded as J D Wetherspoon's the following year.

The legend goes that Martin named Wetherspoon's after his old PE teacher. That means my pub chain would be called Stovalds, which sounds more like an ironmongers. My other games teacher was called Potter, but that would sound like a wizarding theme pub. Intriguingly, the J D part came from Boss Hogg's initials from The Dukes of Hazzard. Another story goes that he named the pub after an old teacher who couldn't keep control of his class, in which case my pub chain would be The Supply Teacher.

By 1986 Martin had amassed a dozen pubs in London. In 1993 he opened pubs further afield in Bracknell and Norwich. Wetherspoon's soon became a nationwide phenomenon. Its empire now holds over 900 pubs, 250 of which have been named in CAMRA's *Good Beer Guide*.

The Gastropub

Aside from the introduction of themed pubs, Irish pubs, Australian pubs and super pubs, the '90s also brought us the gastropub.

Since the 1990s there has been more focus on pub food, with some pubs offering a separate dining room for larger parties to dine. The term gastropub was coined in 1991 when The Eagle in London's Farringdon decided to go gourmet and provide fine dining in a pub. The owners Michael Belben and David Eyre were restaurateurs who wanted to open their own restaurant, but the London rents were too high. However it was now easier to obtain a pub licence, so why not combine the two? Besides which, a restaurant required a certain level of fixtures and fittings, whereas pubgoers are less fussy about decor and the sense of occasion. I like The Eagle's mantra, Never forget it's a pub, which means the menu is black-board-based and seating unreserved. Here there is no preten-tiousness, just good, locally sourced food served with a pint in a pub environment.

Twenty six years on and The Eagle is still going strong. However the term gastropub has become naff and editors of *The Good Food Guide* decided, in their infinite wisdom, to stop using the term in 2011. The word gastropub always makes me giggle as the word gastro in Australia is an abbreviation of gastroenteritis.

Licensing Laws

Incredibly, the licensing laws set out during World War I stayed for the rest of the century. It was not until the 2003 Licensing Act that the rules were relaxed. When I was a teenager in the early-'90s the licensing laws were still fairly strict, so there was always a mad rush to the bar from 10.30pm. You had to get 'em in before the bar stopped serving.

At the time, the tabloid press warned us of the dangers of 24-hour drinking, as if every day would be like Sodom and Gomorrah. But the laws were only changed to stagger every-one's drinking, so we didn't end up in the ridiculous situation of everyone being tipped out of a pub at the same time, boozed up and with testosterone bouncing off the walls. No wonder there was disorder. As someone who works nights, I don't go to pubs until a lot later in the evening, and it means I can still have a night out after hours. Result.

Micropubs

Where do we go after super pubs? Micropubs of course. History is always cyclical. One of the clauses in the 2003

Licensing Act introduced the concept of obtaining a personal licence, which made it possible to convert a retail unit into a micropub. This legislation had huge impact. Martyn Hillier was famously the first person to do so, when he converted an off-licence into The Butchers Arms in Herne, on the Kent coast, and the first micropub was born. He opened the pub as soon as the legislation became active in 2005.

Hillier runs the whole operation himself, selling good quality draught ale, opening when he wants, and keeping his takings just below the VAT threshold. The Butcher's Arms has been a triumph, gaining notice by being awarded CAMRA Kent Pub of the Year 2009, and in 2015 Hillier was named CAMRA Campaigner of the Year. His campaigning included a keynote speech at the CAMRA 2009 AGM on how to set up your own micropub. A few folk took heed and shortly after the Rat Race Alehouse in Hartlepool and Just Beer in Newark were born. It was a huge turning point.

In 2014 the Micropub Association was set up by Hillier and Stu Hirst, as a resource for other would-be micropublicans. There are currently 307 micropubs listed on the website as of November 2017. Interestingly, they define a micropub as:

> *'A small freehouse which listens to its customers, mainly serves cask ales, promotes conversation, shuns all forms of electronics and dabbles in traditional pub snacks.'*

I am sure George Orwell would have agreed wholeheartedly. The 2003 Licensing Act was as important as the 1830 Beerhouse Act. It also enabled microbreweries to set up their own microbrew pubs with a personal license. This is of course nothing new, as it harks back to the original alehouses and brewhouses of the Middle Ages. I wonder which hipster will be the first person to call themselves a brewster?

The Present-Day Struggle

In 2010 the government appointed the first Pubs Minister. John Healy, MP for Wentworth, was handed the inaugural role with a task to head up a strategy to save Britain's pubs. Meanwhile I began drafting my new sitcom, *Yes Pub Minister*.

The political spotlight indeed helped, as the Chancellor duly cut beer duty in 2014 and 2015, and in 2016 it was frozen. However, in the 2017 budget Philip Hammond announced a 2p-a-pint increase in beer duty, the first rise in five years. All is not lost; in a move to save our high-street pubs, he slashed 90% of all bills by £1,000.

Heritage Listed Pubs, ACVs and Co-ops

CAMRA have been very proactive in protecting our pubs, and set up The Pub Heritage Group to raise awareness. Alongside declaring certain older pubs as heritage listed buildings, this group began compiling the national inventory of historic pub interiors. They began in 1991, and currently list 266 pubs. To qualify, the pub interiors have to have been kept largely intact since 1945.

This is fantastic, but what about all those pubs in peril, which were built post-1945? Well, these can be listed as an Asset of Community Value, or ACV. CAMRA defines an ACV as:

> *'Land or property of importance to a local community which is subject to additional protection from development under the Localism Act 2011.'*

These assets can be nominated by a voluntary or local organisation. Once registered, they are protected by the local authority. If the pub owner wishes to sell the pub, the community get first refusal, and they have an option to buy their local pub, under the 'community right to bid' provisions of the Localism Act. Perhaps the most important power is that the sale is paused for six months, giving a potential Co-op time to form and raise funds.

In 2017, 37 years after setting up the CAMRA Pub Protection Group, there was great news for the future of our pubs. According to CAMRA:

> 'After years of campaigning, in July 2017 the Government changed the law... to protect all pubs in England through the planning system. This means that... no pub can be demolished or converted into another use without the say of... the local community.'

Power to the pub people!

Community Pubs

My current local pub, the Ivy House in Nunhead, South-East London, is no ordinary pub, it is the UK's first co-operatively owned pub. Its twitter handle still reads @Save_Ivy_House. The locals, with the help of CAMRA, were able to secure a Grade II listing, as their wonderful wooden interior was largely unchanged since 1945. They were the first pub in London to achieve ACV status. The listing was granted in April 2012, two days before the building was due to be closed down, its wooden interior dismantled, and the pub turned into residential flats. The Ivy House Co-op raised a whopping one million pounds and were able to buy it before their six months' grace period expired. I am happy to say that there are now over 70 community run pubs in the UK. Let's hope that number keeps climbing.

The Ivy House is a community-centric dog-friendly pub, and has a beautiful Victorian-style ballroom, which hosts a variety of functions. I recently utilised the space to promote a comedy night, raising money for a local dog charity. The first time I had a pint in the Ivy House was a Tuesday night. In the front bar, there were locals enjoying a pint, while the ballroom played host to a practising jazz band and a weekly knitting circle. It is a good example of a pub tailoring itself to the community.

Creating and maintaining a successful pub is much harder than it looks. You can't just open the front door and hope folk flock in, like a Boxing Day sale. In these troubled times customers need to be wooed and wowed, and pubs need to adapt to the needs of the modern customer. If pubs are able to change and learn the lessons of history, they will not only survive, but thrive.

GEORGE ORWELL AND THE GENESIS OF THE PUB MANIFESTO

3

GEORGE ORWELL is world famous for such literary classics as *1984* and *Animal Farm*, but, for fanatics of the English pub, he is the man responsible for dreaming up another utopia, a Pubtopia, where all pubs 'are equal, but some are more equal than others.'

The Moon Under Water

George Orwell's vision of the perfect pub, which I touched upon in the last chapter, was immortalised in the creation of his own perfect pub, The Moon Under Water. This was not part of a book, but a short essay. Orwell had been commissioned to write a weekly column in the Saturday edition of the *London Evening Standard*. He chose to write a variety of essays concerning aspects of British life, including how to make a good cup of tea. This was before the invention of the tea bag and phrases like 'Fancy a brew?' and 'Builders' tea with two.'

'The Moon Under Water' was his last essay in the series and his most famous. He wrote it in February 1946. He was 42 years old, the same age as I was when I started writing this book. There comes a time in a man's life when he simply must write a book on pubs. This was not my middle-life crisis, like skateboarding to work – which I have done, badly I might add. This was a calling.

George Orwell

What drew George Orwell to write about pubs? Orwell felt pubs were 'A symbol of working class life that he tended to sentimentalise,' claimed D. J. Taylor, in his acclaimed biography *Orwell: The Life*. You just know that he would have embraced the romantic ideal of the community pub and the micropub movement.

George Orwell was a fascinating individual. Here are six facts about the great man you may not know:

1   His real name was Eric Blair. George Orwell was a nom de plume, conceived to create a more English sounding name. He did this by joining the monarch of the time, George V, with the river Orwell in Suffolk. If Eric Blair were alive today he might have chosen Charles Mersey, William Tyne, or Harry Thames, although the latter sounds like a pretty dodgy geezer.

2   Aldous Huxley, author of *Brave New World*, taught Orwell at Eton. Incredible to think of one great dystopian novelist teaching another, at the same school. I suppose not that incredible, when you consider that school was Eton. What subject did Huxley teach? French! I presume his class tackled existentialist subjects like the philosophy of Sartre rather than humdrum phrases such as 'Le supermarché ferme à midi.'

3   The torture chamber in *1984*, Room 101, was inspired by a dreary room at the BBC where Orwell had to sit through dull meetings during World War II. Incredible to think this ultimately led to a BBC comedy show, currently hosted by Frank Skinner. My book is actually the opposite of the television show, because we are deliberating which parts of pub culture to keep.

4   According to the website of The Canonbury Tavern (a pub in Islington, North London): 'George Orwell, who lived in Canonbury Square, wrote part of *1984* whilst sitting under the tree in the garden in the 1940s.' This makes it sound like he knocked out one of the 20th-century's most defining novels while sipping a cider in the afternoon sunshine. No wonder folk dream of being writers!

5   Orwell allegedly popularised the term 'The Cold War' in an article entitled 'You and The Atomic Bomb' in 1945.
6   *1984* was published in 1949 on the eve of Orwell's death. Not a bad use of the last day of your life.

Genesis of the Perfect Pub Comedy Show

In 2014 I sat in my own garden, with various drinks, and wrote a stand-up comedy show for the Camden and Edinburgh Fringes entitled 'Wine, Ale and I'. It was a fun pun on the cult classic film *Withnail and I*, which seemed apt, as my run kicked off in Camden, Withnail's home territory. In the show I talked about wine, beer and growing up in a pub.

Stand-up audiences have a limited concentration span. Most comedy clubs book acts for 20 minutes. Apparently that is the average time it takes someone to drink a pint. Fringe audiences tend to have a concentration span of about 40 minutes; maybe they are slower drinkers? Whatever the reason, the hardest part of performing a one-hour solo show is tackling that 40-minute lull in concentration. I did so with a bit of audience participation, inspired by George Orwell's perfect pub essay.

Orwell's essay came up with a 10-point plan for the perfect pub. Which begs the question, What would you have in your perfect pub? I would go around the room and ask the audience for their suggestions and riff off their replies. This audience-interactive section of the show was a big hit. It was also the most fun part of the show to perform, as it led to improvisation and meant each night's performance was slightly different.

In January 2015 I toured a version of the show in Australia. I re-branded it 'A Brit's Guide To Booze', a less subtle title, which I thought would appeal to our Aussie brethren. Does exactly what it says on the tin mate.

Weirdly, at Perth Fringe, the PR people said they had great difficulty in promoting the show on television and radio, as the powers that be were worried they might be seen to be promoting booze. Wait a second, promoting booze? This was a show set in the busiest Irish pub in the party city of Perth. I don't think any of my audience needed any encouragement. At least the landlord of my venue, Rosie O'Grady's, was happy with the amount my audience drank at each show. Again, fuelled by alcohol, the audience participation section was the best part of the show.

The Aussie tour ended with a show at one of my favourite breweries, Little Creatures. It does a fantastic pale ale which in my opinion is even better than Cooper's in the mass market. While touring Freemantle, I hosted a comedy wine tasting one afternoon. Unfortunately I had a problem; many of the audience had also bought tickets to my evening show. Alas, I had already used my best material on booze in the afternoon. Without wishing to repeat material, there was only one option: trial a new hour show riffing on the perfect pub. It worked, and I felt confident enough to present it as a full show.

Perth taught me that if you are doing a show about pubs, it is best to base it in the busiest one. So I booked a month's slot at The Three Sister's pub in Edinburgh.

I spent the next few months reading every book, news-paper and internet article I could find about pubs. My life was a virtual pub crawl. At this time, *How I Escaped My Certain Fate*, by the comedian Stewart Lee, was the only non-pub book on my Kindle. I remember my fiancée Leo and I were relaxing on a Thai beach and all I could talk about was the state of British pubs. Which is ironic, as when I am at my local pub in South London, I am often tucking into a Chicken Massaman curry and dreaming wistfully of Thailand.

I performed a variety of practice shows known as Edinburgh previews. My first was in The Comedy Pub, just off Piccadilly Circus, which meant the audience was populated with tourists. In fact the front row was Greek. I was relieved to realise that the demise and subsequent deification of pubs was a universal subject; however not many internationals knew about George Orwell, 'The Moon Under Water', or indeed Wetherspoon. Still, the Greeks were intrigued by what they referred to as this 'spoon-themed pub' and endeavoured to make a pilgrimage to find one.

The Edinburgh Fringe Festival

I conducted my show in a pub venue at the Edinburgh Fringe Festival, so I should give you a brief contextual background. The first time I visited Edinburgh was in 1997, for an aggressively titled new act stand-up competition called 'So You Think You're Funny.'

The first thing that struck me about Edinburgh was that peculiar apple-pie smell. I initially thought that may be why Edinburgh is known as 'Auld Reekie'. I was informed it is actually an old Scottish nickname, meaning Old Smoky, and referred to the smoke rising from the tenements. The modern apple-pie smell emanates from hops from the Caledonian Brewery, which gives us the delectable Deuchars IPA and, more recently, Three Hop lager.

Referring to the smell, I would quip: "It's as if the brewery is sending us a subliminal message: 'Don't worry, we're making more beer.'" My second observation on arrival was that, even at 10pm, my host was in no rush to head to the pub. "Pubs up here don't really get started until 10.30," my friend declared.

The licensing laws in Scotland used to be more relaxed, especially during the fringe festival. It was a cold August night, pitch black to the south and strangely light towards the north, as a result of it being that much closer to the Arctic Circle. We walked into a bustling smoke den of a pub on Victoria Street, just off The Grassmarket.

"Pint of mild or a pint of heavy?" asked my host.
"Heavy please."

I didn't know what heavy was, but when has mild been a good thing? Turns out heavy is Eighty Shilling and a lot stronger than the Sixty. Needless to say, I slept well that night.

Fast forward to Edinburgh 2015, where I bounced between four pubs. My venue, The Three Sisters, on Cowgate, is one of the largest pubs in the city. It has a huge screen housed in an outdoor courtyard, making it a magnet for stags, hens and sports fans. They even sell beer and cider in two-pint pots. This was the drinking gene pool from which some of my audience might emanate. Strap in I thought, it might be a lively fringe.

A few doors down from the Three Sisters is BrewDog, the popular Aberdonian craft beer house famous for its anarchic beers, from Punk IPA to Tactical Nuclear Penguin. There is also Bannerman's, a locals' pub and a favourite watering hole for rockers. Embracing the metal scene, I drank Trooper, produced by Bruce Dickinson from the band Iron Maiden. My favourite pub was The Halfway House, aptly named as it is tiny public house, half-way down a flight of stone steps, between The Royal Mile and Waverley Station. Full it would fit about 30 folk and it has the atmosphere of a large living room. The Halfway House keeps a sensational cellar and is a keen supporter of local breweries.

I stayed with four other comics, in a flat at the foot of Leith walk. It was a formerly rough area, now gentrified and made famous by Irvine Welsh's novels and the Proclaimers' song 'Sunshine On Leith.' Near our flat was a pub that shall be nameless, the roughest pub I'd ever seen. It should have had a bloodied plaque on the wall. It looked like a betting shop with a bar, and the kind of place where one could purchase a gun. Its clientele were those who felt the nearby Wetherspoon's was far too fancy. During my Fringe run, I used this pub as the antithesis of the Perfect Pub.

My show concept was simple. After a preamble explaining the sad state of pub closures and the reasons why, I would ask the members of the audience questions individually as to what makes their perfect pub. Ordinarily, if you ask an open question in a comedy club, it will be answered by one of the more confident, or most alcohol-assisted people, in the room. By asking questions individually you get more interesting feedback, as the quiet ones often give a more thoughtful answer than the shouty, impulsive, noisy ones.

After a few shows, I realised the direction or indeed the vibe of the show would be dictated by that opening suggestion. Sometimes it would be a straightforward "Good beer," or "Log fire," but in September 2015 in Camden the opening gambit was "Jousting!" This was an inspired suggestion, which set a delightfully surreal tone to the show.

Suggestions I liked, or ones that were popular with the crowd, were chalked up on a blackboard. After each show I would take a photograph of the blackboard as a record and a reminder.

On the last night of the end of the festival, I was carrying my blackboard out of a pub and was accused by a bouncer of stealing items of pub property. When I revealed why I was carrying it, he and his mate thought long and hard, before concluding that heaters in the doorway were required in their perfect pub.

Raw Data Revealed

A week into the run, my friend Philippa Moffat came to see the show and suggested it might make a good subject for a book. We pondered over a pint and realised that, unbeknownst to me, I had actually been doing my own research on what makes the perfect pub. These audience suggestions were not just fodder for comedy, but actual data.

As I had a photographic record of the previous show suggestions, I logged these and all future suggestions in a notebook. It was no ordinary notebook; it was a present from

Leo, a black leather-bound journal, with my name embossed.
I hope she was not charged for the embossing by the letter, as
the length of my surname would make it pretty expensive.

Without further ado, here is the data collated from my
Edinburgh Fringe audience over a period of 21 shows:

Suggestion	Number of Shows Suggested (out of 21)
Good Beer	21
Wine	13
Sofa/Comfy Seats	13
Pool Table (ideally free)	12
Jukebox/Good Music	12
Quiz Night	11
Pub Dog	10
Roaring Fire	8
Live Music	8
Good Food	8
Good Snacks	8
Good Gin Selection	8
Free Ride Home	6
Good Whisky Selection	6
No Kids	6
Pub Garden	6
Friendly Customers/Regulars	4
TV	4
Cocktails	4
Darts	4
Karaoke	3
Nice Toilets/Toilet Roll	3
Table Tennis Table	3
No Wi-Fi	2
Scenic View	2
Jousting	1

I should reiterate that this data was courtesy of audience interaction during a live show, so the information provided was what the participant felt comfortable or confident enough to share aloud. For example, I imagine good toilets, or at least a plentiful supply of loo roll, would feature a lot higher on a confidential survey.

Looking at the data, there are no surprises in seeing good beer and wine topping the charts. Gin and whisky were also a fairly popular request. Whisky's popularity may have been due to my being in Scotland, whereas if I perform the show in South-West England cider becomes more prominent. Comfortable seating scored highly; this might have something to do with the recent hard furnishing trend in pubs, and folk wishing for a return to softer decor. (More on this in Chapter 5.) I am quite surprised by how popular the pool table is, although that is one game most people cannot play at home.

In July 2017, YouGov Omnibus conducted their own research. According to their survey, the single most important feature of the Britons' ideal pub is serving meals (67%). Whereas my comedy crowd would probably pipe up "Eating's cheating!"

A good beer garden secured their second-highest vote, with 63%. This only received 6 votes in my survey; however, mine was conducted in Scotland, where a beer garden is perhaps challenged by the weather. Also, how many of these people surveyed were really pub people? Their primary needs seem to be eating outside; maybe they would be happier reclining in an restaurant, al fresco.

Interestingly, in the government survey the pool table was comparable with a bookcase full of books, suggesting they may have been targeting a rather middle-class crowd. I used to work in a Waterstones bookstore and would therefore often have a book on my person. If I arrived in a pub before my friends, I would pull out a book and read over a pint. In one local bar I got the nickname 'The Reader'.

Whatever the stats show, it is incredible to think that one small essay, written in 1946, is still having ramifications today. There is a newspaper article every six months or so dedicated to George Orwell and his perfect pub. They all write about Orwell's formula and how it applies today, but do not really have the time, or the luxury, to explore the subject in any great depth. This book intends to answer definitively what we should do to save our beloved boozers from demise and perhaps even extinction. Now, let us create the perfect pub from scratch, starting with the location.

With John Hatch, Head brewer at Ram Brewery, right after a performance of my Perfect Pub stand-up show.

PUB LOCATION, PUB LOCATION, PUB LOCATION

4

I N HIS ESSAY 'The Moon Under Water' George Orwell opens by addressing the location of his proposed perfect pub:

> *'My favourite public-house, the Moon Under Water,*
> *is only two minutes from a bus stop, but it is on a*
> *side-street, and drunks and rowdies never seem to*
> *find their way there, even on Saturday nights.'*

Orwell sought a slightly secluded pub, off the beaten track, yet with reasonable transport links. We all like to discover a hidden gem, rather than wander blindly into the harsh lights of a high-street establishment. Especially one containing 'Rowdies.'

Years ago, I met a friend for a pint at The Compton Arms in Islington. It was slightly hard to find as it was tucked down a side street. However, it was still a short walk from a bus stop, and Highbury and Islington tube station. It was a cold, wet Wednesday evening, but once inside we were greeted with a warm hearth and a welcoming atmosphere. The walls were adorned with pictures and clippings of George Orwell. Had we inadvertently stumbled into his perfect pub? The pub certainly celebrated Orwell drinking there.

Orwell lived at 27b Canonbury Square in Islington from 1944 to 1947, during which time he allegedly frequented three

Islington pubs: The Compton Arms, The Canonbury, and The Hen and Chickens. The latter was even the inspiration for his proletarian pub in his novel *1984*. It is worth noting that although Orwell's ideal is cherished by most pub enthusiasts, it really only discusses the concerns of a city pub. After all, the article was commissioned by a London newspaper.

Apart from city pubs, there are three other main location types to consider: country pubs, coastal and waterside, and railway pubs.

Country Pubs

My dad bought his pub in 1969. It was the summer of love and my dad loved pubs. While he was area manager for Berni Inns, my father realised he was spending all his time and wages in pubs, so why not invest in his own establishment? This gave him what the Sunday supplements love to refer to as a good work-life balance.

Once my father decided he wished to buy a country pub, he enlisted a few friends to act as scouts. Pub scout must list as one of my ultimate jobs, along with wine taster, monkey handler and England football manager. All you need is a copy of the *Good Beer Guide*, Google Maps and a thirst. Of course, in the late '60s they would have scrutinised a road atlas, searching for that sacred symbol, a red PH. It took them two whole years to find a suitable pub; quite right too. Being a pub scout is a long-term project, a task to savour, not rush; like trying to get pregnant, there is no point in hitting the jackpot first time.

The criteria for my father's perfect pub was simple: it had to be a free house in the countryside but on the edge of a burgeoning community. Back then free houses – that is to say pubs independently owned and not tied to a brewery – were even scarcer than they are now. This meant he could be his own boss and not be subservient to the whims, beer choices and rent hikes of a big brewer.

The pub he eventually chose was The Anchor Inn, Oldbury-on-Severn. It is a small village pub nestled on the banks of the River Severn, 10 miles north of Bristol. It dates back to Roman times. In fact there are still remains of a Roman camp at the top of the village. The previous owner was a chap called Edmund Grace, nephew of famous cricketer and prodigious drinker W. G. I imagine the batting crease wasn't the only place he'd refuse to leave after time was called.

There are some incredible country pubs all over the UK, but you cannot be too far off the grid. You still need to be near a focal point, whether it is a local town, a major road, a place of interest, a good walk or a natural beauty spot. There is less passing trade in the country so a steady stream of locals is required to prop up the bar. In the early days, my dad would often wander up and down the high street of the local town, drumming up trade.

People love motoring out to a country pub; however, the drink-driving laws mean a designated driver is required. Gone are the wild days of the '60s and '70s, when tractors were heaving cars out of ditches. On the plus side, as a country pub is harder to reach, customers will often have a meal too, rather than pass through after one or two pints, as they may do in a city pub.

Pubs by Water

Aside from the countryside, people love drinking by water, whether that be riverside, lakeside, canalside or coastal.

For a short time my dad owned the tenancy on a beautiful pub called The Boat, in Redbrook, just past Tintern Abbey. I loved it. It had two distinguishing features. Firstly, the car park was in England and the pub was in Wales. There was a footbridge that took you across the River Wye and acted as border control. Secondly, the pub garden was cut into the rock face and overlooking the Wye. There are picnic tables on ledges with tiny waterfalls streaming in between. Canoeists would moor up and grab a pint or a spot of lunch before continuing paddling down to Tintern Abbey, or up to Monmouth.

I once camped on the side of the river with two childhood friends, Si and Steve. Before we left my Mum insisted I take two sleeping bags, just in case. "Why does anyone need two?" the boys asked. They ribbed me incessantly and referred to me as Jimmy 'two sleeping bags'. Our plan was to have a few pints and then camp overnight. Most normal folk would erect the tent first, then pop next door for a pint. Not us. After a skinful, we went to unload our gear. I put the first sleeping bag down, and as I reached for the second, the first rolled into the water. I heard the splash, but it was pitch black, so it was impossible to find it. I am so glad my Mum had the foresight to remind me to take two. Never ignore the wisdom of mums.

My favourite canalside pub is actually in the heart of the Birmingham, our version of Venice. Broad Street is the Saturday night strip, where hordes of stags and hens prowl the pubs and clubs, like majestic beasts hunting on the Serengeti. However, if you duck down Gas Street you will stumble across a 19th-century canalside pub called The Tap and Spile. It has a welcoming atmosphere and a delightful selection of real ales, which you can drink peacefully, overlooking the canal, far from the madding crowd of Broad Street.

Coastal Pubs

Seaside pubs are usually heaving when the sun comes out. Personally, I prefer a coastal pub in winter. A couple of years ago, I spent a weekend in Cornwall for a friends' 40th. It was mid-November and we headed to Trebarwith Strand beach, two miles south of Tintagel. It is renowned for its long stretch of golden sand. Unfortunately, as we entered at Port William cove, there was a storm brewing. The weather was bracing, horizontal rain and high winds, rendering umbrellas useless. Some of the more adventurous in our party stripped off and braved the crashing sea. They emerged shivering and blue, like scared Smurfs. Olly, the birthday boy, suggested we take shelter in the Port William pub, overlooking the cove. There is something wonderful about escaping the sea-salted blustery elements, and taking shelter in a warm pub, by the fire. Rainstorms are delightful, as long as you are the right side of a pane of glass, nursing a pint of something interesting.

Railway Pubs

Like British seaside towns, railway pubs were very popular in the last century. Up until the 1960s beer was transported on the railways, which is why my dad reckons, historically speaking, you were almost guaranteed a good pint at a railway station pub.

With railway stations revitalising, the pubs inside are making a resurgence. The publisher of this book, Simon Hall, introduced me to the Parcel Yard at King's Cross station. It is a short hop, skip and a jump from the famous Platform 9¾. On my first visit, I had to part a queue of Harry Potter fans just to get to the pub. The Parcel Yard is a beautiful Fuller's pub, located in an old Grade I listed Great Northern Railway sorting office and embracing all the classic features of train travel: luggage racks, old patterned train seats, historic signs, train memorabilia and, fortunately during my visit, no delays at the bar.

Another fine example of a beautiful railway pub is The Sheffield Tap. Local entrepreneurs Jamie Hawksworth and Jon Holdsworth, who already owned a café bar in York, saw the potential in the dilapidated Grade II listed building, lying dormant and used for storage, at Sheffield station. It was originally an ornate bar and resting rooms for First Class passengers, dating back to 1904. According to Jamie, in an article in the *Sheffield Telegraph* on 1 October 1989:

> *'It was at least six feet deep in rubbish when we took it over. The ceiling had collapsed. It was in a sorry state.'*

Thanks to a grant from the Railway Heritage Trust and backing from Thornbridge Brewery, one person's rubbish became another's treasure. You can now have a cracking night out in Sheffield without ever leaving the train station.

Thornbridge director Simon Webster gives a financial perspective:

'We calculated what the through-put of beer would be by the end of the year and we exceeded it within three months. It was phenomenal – 100,000 people pass through the station every week. If you get 1% of those, you've got a thousand people, but it's become far more than that'. (This interview was from a wonderfully titled article, 'Campaign for Rail Ale', in *The Guardian* by Tony Naylor in June 2010.)

Here the location is paramount and the figures seem to add up to a fine investment.

The majestic Sheffield Tap, at Sheffield railway station

The Centurion, in Newcastle, is equally impressive. Like the Sheffield Tap, it was formerly a First Class waiting room. It was originally built in 1893 and lovingly restored in 2001. I went there on a stag do with my brothers-in-law, after a day at the cricket, and was surprised by how plush it was. In hindsight, I am glad we just went there for our first couple of pints, rather than the head-spinning tail-enders. According to the barman, in the 1960s it was used by the British Transport Police as cells. Now that is what I call a proper lock-in.

Another success story, on a different scale, is The Rat Race Ale House, situated on the platform of Hartlepool railway station. It was the first micropub on Teeside, first opening its doors in 2009, and was named CAMRA's North-East pub of the year in 2013. The Rat Race's website reports they have served: 'Different beers from 451 different breweries since opening day (25th November 2009) – and counting!' That is a magnificent effort and just shows how passionate and versatile a micropub can be.

However these pub triumphs are few and far between. The Beer House (previously known as the Nor' Loch) at Edinburgh Waverley, the White Star Bar at Liverpool Lime Street, and the White Rose at Leeds stations, are all fairly basic. Since my last visit, Edinburgh has added The Booking Office, above the station, which Wetherspoon's opened in March 2016. Birmingham New Street has an All Bar One, Manchester Piccadilly is reasonably well served with the Mayfield Bar, but they are hardly in the same league as the majestic Sheffield Tap, the innovative Rat Race, the classic Centurion or the imperious Parcel Yard.

Nottingham railway station, Cardiff Central and Bristol Temple Meads are all sadly lacking in bars and expect you to seek solace in the nearby city-centre drinking establishments. Where are the glorious pubs at London Victoria and Clapham Junction to lift the spirits of a comatose commuter?

With the HS2 and HS3 train projects seeking to link up the north and south of England with a swifter line, how about a few decent pubs to welcome those weary travellers? Besides, the time saved on train travel can be spent wisely in a good pub. Maybe we should take Tony Naylor's *Guardian* piece literally and start a Campaign for Rail Ale.

Extreme Locations

The UK's highest pub is The Tan Hill Inn, in North Yorkshire; it is 1732 feet above sea level. They are quite literally off the grid and have a mobile generator to prove it.

The Dragon's Back is the highest pub I have drunk in recently, a mere 1000 feet above sea level. It is not a Lord of the Rings theme bar, but a pub in the Brecon Beacons. Saying that, they did have a fun signpost outside, directing you to various fantasy locations including Winterfell, Rivendell and Mordor. Perhaps, with the Marvel Comics film franchise gathering pace, it will not be long before there is a Lord of the Thrones mash up.

I stayed at The Dragon's Back while on a walking trip of the Brecon Beacons, celebrating my friend Hippy Jim's impending fatherhood. My fellow Swansea Uni mates and I were greeted by Amed, who has not only been the landlord for 20 years, but whose previous job was a stand-up comedian. There is hope for me yet! The rain was pelting the window panes, but the fire was roaring inside. We shook off the rain like wet dogs and ordered a round. Five pints of delicious Butty Bach (Wye Valley Brewery) came to an astonishing £17! I don't want to sound like a city boy on safari, but that's a bargain. What's more, our lodgings were only £22 per night.

The Dragon's Back is a great example a pub maximising its location. They have two adjoining bunkhouses sleeping 10 apiece, plus a couple of glamping lodges. There was one designed like the Tardis – the outside, not the inside! All of us ate and drank in the pub. Besides Butty Bach, there is also Wye Valley's 1985 lager, and the hoppy but thirst-quenching Chinook craft beer on tap. Why would you drink anywhere else?

On the Saturday night, I even bumped into my former head brewer, from when I worked at Smiles Brewery, in Bristol. Richard was sampling a post-walk ale too. The pub world is a small convivial one.

The lowest pub in England is the Admiral Wells in Peterborough, which is 9 feet below sea level. Admittedly the lowest pub is not quite as sexy or glamorous as an underground bar. One of the quirkiest is Manchester's Temple of Convenience, so called because it is housed in an old public convenience. The lead singer of Elbow, Guy Garvey, immortalised it in his song 'Grounds for Divorce' which contains the lyric:

> *'There's a hole in my neighbourhood down which of late*
> *I cannot help but fall.'*

There are actually a few pubs in former toilets, but this is the only one folk have sung about.

If you are really looking for remote, The Marisco Tavern might be for you. It is situated on Lundy Island, 12 miles off the coast of north Devon. There is a small airfield, but those of us who aren't international playthings, or Bond villains, have to content ourselves with a two-hour ferry boat ride from Bideford. Such a pity it doesn't leave from the gangster cove of Westward Ho!

Regardless of location, I like being able to walk to a pub. The journey there is full of joyful anticipation, and the jaunt home is perfect for clearing the head before bed. While at Swansea University I lived on top of a steep hill and would scamper down to a pub called The Woodman. After a few pints the sheer walk home somehow seemed easier. After all, they say the best way to climb a steep hill is to avoid going in a straight line.

INTERIOR DESIGN, DARLING

5

THE FIRST THING I look for when I walk into a pub is the bar. It is the focal point of any pub.

When my Dad bought The Anchor in 1969 it had three separate bars: two public bars and one lounge bar. The first change he made was to install an open-plan bar so he could entertain both the lounge and public bars at once. This is commonplace now, but fairly innovative at the time.

I like a simple bar layout, where I can easily scan and assess all the drinks options on offer. There was a ridiculous trend in the '90s for huge beer fount towers, each emblazoned with advertising. Big breweries tried to dominate the marketplace with their monstrous monoliths, like a race to build the tallest skyscraper. Some were so big, the bar staff had to lean around, or between them, just to talk to a customer.

Log Fire

A good log fire is a timeless pleasure and, apart from the promise of liquor, was one of the foremost attractions of a public house in olden times. With the advent of central heating, a pub fireplace is a luxury, rather than a necessity. It is a treat to defrost our feet and warm the cockles on a cold winter's day. (Writing this, I have just realised that cockles is cockney rhyming slang for muscles, and not as saucy as I had previously suspected.)

The romantic glow of a fireside gives a pub focus, and brightens the atmosphere of even the dullest room. There is nothing like cradling a pint, or cupping a mulled wine, while gazing wistfully into the flickering flames. A good fire is mesmeric and hypnotic. I also love the dying embers at the end of a good night.

As a kid I liked collecting kindling, but the most fun was poking at a fire unnecessarily, prompting sparks and watching the logs buckle and crack. I remember my Action Man doll fell in our pub fireplace once. Turns out his army uniform was as flammable as the average 1980s tracksuit, and he was soon down to his plastic undies. It made my sister's Barbie doll blush.

One pub near me is called The Pyro's Arms, which pretty much guarantees the presence of a good fireplace.

In recent times some bars have started playing a DVD recording of a fireplace on their TV screens. This may soothe Homer Simpson, but the rest of us need a little more substance. Whatever next – a DVD recording of a full moon at midnight, or the sun coming up when you want to kick the punters out? Actually, that is not such a crazy idea.

Pub Furniture

Most pub furniture tends to be wooden; what else would you surround a roaring log fire with in winter?

Also, why is that most pub chairs look like they've been rescued from an old Methodist church, village hall or abandoned Cub Scout hut? Perhaps the hymn book holders could double up for mobile phone sheaths or shot-glass shelves.

A quick browse at the pub furniture outlets on the internet revealed various variations of pub chair:

1 'The Straight Leg Mates Chair' – a seat for blokes who sport a particular trouser cut. What about the 'skinny jean stool' for those who can't sit down, as their trousers are too tight?

2 'The Straight Leg Captain's Chair' – similar to the above, but with a rounded back. It is often seen in seaside taverns and bars.

3 'The Admiral's Chair' – popular with Lord Nelson, so watch you don't poke your eye out.

As they all have a naval bent, I am relieved to realise that the word mates is short for shipmates. A range of pub chairs aimed solely at lads and geezers would be too much to bear. Other styles include the 'Fiddleback', 'Spindleback' and 'Slatback', which all sound like dusty wooden board games from ye olden days.

Usually the only non-wooden item is the ubiquitous battered leather Chesterfield sofa. I feel sorry for all the other sofas styles, despite being on sale throughout the year; they never get to hang out at the pub like their leather counterparts. The last time I was sprawled on a Chesterfield, I stuck my hand down the side and entered a netherworld. You're wrong to wince dear reader. I found two iPhone handsets, £3.62 and a furry fluff-ridden fruit pastille. This netherworld became my nirvana.

When drinking in a country pub, my Dad used to insist I stand at the bar. He claims by standing you can be more mobile, and able to ebb and flow between conversations, whereas if you sit down you don't know who might sit next to you.

Most girls, by contrast, love to sit down. They have a spider-sense when it comes to spotting a free table. They are on it like a flash, so quick it borders on teleportation. How many times have we heard the phrase "Mind if we jump in your grave?" However, if you time it wrong, you can end up in someone's lap, which is embarrassing.

We do require comfortable chairs. Some people have back problems and need a little extra luxury. So it is worthwhile having a few higher-quality chairs, for added comfort and support, for those who need it. There is nothing like languishing in a comfy chair, and supping a pint, while reading a newspaper, book or scrolling through your smartphone.

Bar stools are a must; you can sit, but still be where the action is. Beware sitting on a stool in a local's pub, as it might belong to a particular farmer or postman. My rule is, if you can see a buttock print or indentation, leave well alone. Bar stools should be spaced out around the bar. There is nothing worse than a barrier of bar stools blocking the bar and slowing down service.

The problem with pub furniture is that it is often weathered, mismatching and rickety. I remember once drinking in a bar in Pontardawe, in South Wales, called The Pink Geranium. They had two pub dogs called Rambo and Wheels – what great names! They sound like two dozy sidekicks from a comedy gangster film. These delightful dogs preferred stool legs to sticks and had almost gnawed their way right through. Every time you sat, you did so gingerly, as there was a chance the legs would crash from beneath you. It was like a cross between playing Jenga and Russian Roulette on bar stools.

Leo is petite. She would like more rungs, so she can climb up like a step ladder, and still have a rung to rest her feet.

Acoustics

One big change is the absence of a sticky carpet. This has been pulled up and replaced with the hardwood floor. This current minimalist trend of clean lines and hardwood floors might look stylish, but the lack of soft furnishings wreaks havoc with the acoustics. With little or no soundproofing, every sound is magnified, and this ruins any precious atmosphere the landlord is trying to create.

5 Steps to Make a Hipster Bar

One of the current trends is the hipster pub. You too can make one in 5 simple steps:

1   Acquire a famously rough pub, in a soon-to-be-gentrified area.

2   Attack the walls with a sander until you reach the original wall but, importantly, only finish two-thirds of the job, so you can still see brickwork peeking out from behind the plaster. It is the same principle as a designer pair of distressed jeans.

3   Rip up the carpet, but keep the old dartboard, pool table and fixtures and fittings.

4   Americanise the bar with old-school neon and low lighting.

5   Finally mount a stag's head on the wall for no reason whatsoever and marvel at 'how random' it is. In fact it is anything but; George Orwell even alluded to '...the stuffed bull's head over the mantelpiece,' and that was back in 1946.

Pub Restoration

Of course, I'm being deliberately cynical here. Some pub companies have turned pub restoration into an art form. Whatever your views on Wetherspoon's, you cannot deny their ability to acquire some beautiful buildings, keep the facade, and embrace the ethos of the original building. Thanks to Wetherspoon's, we have been able to enjoy a pint in such rich locations as former law courts, banks, theatres, cinemas and even churches, where you can worship your pint.

There are even a couple of pubs set in former swimming pools, including the brilliantly named Swim Inn, in Sheffield. I imagine being served a novelty pint with a tiny brick at the bottom. They could install a footbath for those who insist on wearing flip-flops. I would however draw the line at some whacky dude drinking from a snorkel.

My favourite pub company (come on, we've all got one) is Antic. I first discovered them in Tooting in South London.

I don't mean to be London-centric, I am just talking from my own experience. In 2003 Tooting was blessed with the best strip of curry houses outside Brick Lane, but alas, only three or four pubs. My two flatmates, Andy Pank and Hippy Jim, embarked on a Tooting pub crawl and returned 33 minutes later claiming the pubs in question were too rough! As Tooting became gentrified, so too were the pubs and bars. Antic transformed a former tramshed into a funky bar called the Tooting Tram & Social. The original structure is still in place and the steel supporting girders are a now feature, offset by a pair of whopping chandeliers.

Up the road Antic repurposed the Balham Bowling Club. This pub defines Antic: they kept all the original features of the bowling club, and introduced good craft ales and fine pub food. You can drink in the bar, or dine in the members' area of the bowling club. They have done a similar semi-makeover with The Job Centre in Deptford, a former post office in Forest Hill called The Sylvan Post, and the Catford Constitutional Club. It is not a dissimilar model from Wetherspoon's, refitting and renovating intriguing old buildings, but their market seems aimed towards middle-class professionals.

One of my Dad's fellow managers at Berni Inns, in the 1960s, was Michael Cannon, who went on to own various pub chains including Devenish, Morrells, and Eldridge Pope, but made his mark on the pub decoration side. He purchased 273 underperforming managed houses, and closed each one for a few days for a total refurbishment, which changed their atmosphere and character overnight. Hence the name of his organisation, Magic Pub Company.

Michael employed a SWAT team of about 30 plumbers, painters, plasterers and electricians. They would work in teams, 24 hours a day, to fit the pub out with new cellars, toilets, lighting, kitchens and carpets. After which they were decorated with paintings, mirrors, stuffed animals, farming tools, fishing nets and various artefacts. The new décor was very well received by the customers and in most cases lives to this day. The Magic Pub Company was not alone in this style of operation. Irish and Australian theme pubs work in a similar manner.

Clocks

What is the fascination with pub clocks? We loiter and lounge in pubs. They should be places where time stops, refuges where you can relax away from the rat race. Now the licensing laws have been extended there is no need to keep one eye on closing time.

A Brass Rail

A brass rail might look like old-fashioned novelty item but, by adding little hooks, it can be used to hang your coat or bag. You can now buy stylish padlocks, so you can chain your handbag to a chair or bar rail. It is terrible that we have to re-sort to such safety measures, but it does allow us to relax, rather than having to keep a constant eye on our possessions.

A brass rail also allows you to steady the ship if you're starting to gently sway. Nautical trinkets seem to be very popular these days, and not just in seaside pubs. As I have previously mentioned, my Dad's pub is called The Anchor. We have an anchor moored at the front and a few salmon putchers hanging inside, but that's it. Although some pubs go almost literally overboard on the décor, if you'll pardon the expression, with clocks, funny signs, old lamps and various trinkets.

Pub Design Awards

In 1983, CAMRA launched their own Pub Design Awards. Back then there was only one category, Best Pub Refurbishment. This was jointly awarded to The Bricklayers Arms, London and The Britannia Inn, Lancashire. There are now four award categories. The winners in 2017 were:

CONSERVATION: Greenwood Hotel (Northolt, London) – a Grade II listed Wetherspoon's pub. The judges said 'shows how subtlety and respect can often achieve more than big-budget transformation'.

REFURBISHMENT: Fitzroy Tavern (Soho, London) – restored back to its former Victorian splendour.

REFURBISHMENT (highly commended): Board Inn (Bridlington)

CONVERSION: Bowland Beer Hall (Lancashire) – a former textile mill was regenerated by local architect Charles Stanton. It now boasts one of the longest bars in Britain. It is 105ft 4ins long and houses 42 handpulls.

CONVERSION (highly commended): Caley Picture House (Edinburgh)

NEW BUILD: The Sail Loft (Greenwich, London) – an innovative floor to ceiling glass design.

These awards can only help to raise the bar when it comes to pub interior design. It is interesting to note how much effort is being put into the preservation of our pub culture. We want to build for the future without losing touch with the past.

In Summation

After gigging at the Grainstore Brewery Tap, in Oakham, I had a pint with Rory Gibson, Oakham brewer and 'Cellar Goblin'. In an ever-changing world, he summed up the modern eclectic nature of pub décor beautifully:

> *"I love interesting things on the wall*
> *and seeing new things constantly."*

TOILET TALES

6

ONE ITEM George Orwell omitted to discuss in his 'Moon Under Water' essay, was the state of the pub toilet.

In my Perfect Pub show, decent toilets were mentioned fairly regularly, mostly by the girls, although I'm fairly certain more boys would complain too if they had to do a sit-down wee.

Good pub toilets are a must, especially if you have 'broken the seal'. During the Grunge years of the early '90s I recall reading about a pub in Seattle where the drinks were free from a certain time up until the first person went to the loo. That is pee-er pressure.

I also remember hearing that your drinking ability is based on how long you can hold your bladder for. When I was 18 I was out with a few rugby lads from school, and lasted five-and-a-half pints before breaking the seal. Never again; I nearly self-combusted.

The Royal Philharmonic

Arguably, the best and most famous pub toilets are those in The Royal Philharmonic, in Liverpool. The urinals are made of roseate marble. The style is sculpted porcelain art, and they are a wonder to behold. So much so, while I was in the midst of enjoying them, a bus load of Japanese tourists burst in and started taking pictures. Now that's taking the piss.

The Anchor

In The Anchor, we used to have a handyman called Harry. He was in his late 60s and wore a green boiler suit. One of his duties was servicing the loos, and he delighted in giving my Dad daily updates. The one I remember the most was:

> *"Mike, I'm not sure what happened last night,*
> *but judging by the state of the ceiling, you must've*
> *had a troop of acrobats peeing in here."*

My Dad tried to improve the ambience in the ladies loos by putting up a few paintings. All three went missing. So he asked Harry to screw the painting frames into the wall. They still went missing. Does that mean ladies were smuggling in screwdrivers in handbags? At least it explains why girls go in pairs – one to commit the crime, the other on look-out.

Irish Pub Toilets

Irish pub toilets carry the words 'Mna' and 'Fir' on the doors. I have always managed to muddle the two. The problem is 'Mna' suggests an anagram of man and looks like the word male, and 'Fir' implies female, but it's actually the other way around. This does explain why I visited so many ladies loos in Ireland. I can also reveal that ladies talk in the toilets a lot more than men. One asked: "Any paper in yours love?"

That would never happen in the Gents, or the 'Fir'. When I realised my mistake, I immediately sat down. If I remained standing up, and a lady spied my feet pointing in the opposite direction, she would have deduced that either I was a pervert, or double-jointed.

Don't get me wrong, I have had trouble in the 'Fir' too. While travelling around Ireland with my friend, Jonny Dyke, we happened upon a pub called O'Looneys, in Lahinch, on the West Coast of Ireland. It was as eccentric as it sounds. When we asked the landlord when the pub closed, he said: "October."

Johnny bought a round, and I sauntered into the 'Fir.' While I was in there, a wizened old guy, who looked like an ex-jockey, eyed me casually, and said, "Are yous 'avin a piss or going for da main t'ing?"

I stifled a nervous laugh, and wished I had gone in the Ladies again.

The Pub Toilet Manifesto

Here is my 12-point plan for improving the pub toilet:

1   Clean bathrooms. If the toilets are dirty, it makes you question the cleanliness of the kitchen, the beer pipes and the cellar. People might occasionally complain of food poisoning in a pub, but often it is not the meal itself that made their tummy sick, but the germ-infested toilet they visited.

2   Fresh supply of loo paper. As a boy, there is nothing worse than having to order some toilet roll at the bar, and having to parade that loo roll across the room, with everyone knowing what you're about to do. This is especially embarrassing on a date. From a female perspective, no loo paper in the Ladies is criminal.

3   The hot water tap should be in full working order. This is not a nightclub.

4   Fresh soap in the dispenser.

5   A good hand drier. I would appreciate a fairly quiet contraption. Some hand driers are so loud, you can tell when your partner, or friend, is finishing up in the other bathroom. Also, as a comedian, a buzzing hand drier in the bathroom of a comedy club can sabotage a punchline to a joke.

6   The toilets should be clearly signed. I imagine the staff might get fed up with pointing out the whereabouts of the loos all day.

7   A set of toilets on the ground floor; some folk struggle with stairs.

8   Light and airy, ideally with an open window.

9   A working lock on the cubicle door. No peepholes in the cubicle sides.

10 A clean mirror, especially in the ladies.*

11 More than one toilet cubicle in the men's bathroom. Some guys have sensitive issues and require their privacy.

12 Certainly no rapping toilet attendants, spitting rhyming couplets, while trying to palm you off with aftershave, in the vain hope of receiving tips.

By rights this chapter should be short, to the point, and printed on double-quilt paper. I think we need a breath of fresh air. Let us head outside into the beer garden.

---

*I always marvel at how vain some men are in front of a bathroom mirror.
One time, I saw a guy fluffing his hair in the mirror, trying to achieve the casually messed up look. He seemed to be adjusting every strand purposefully to appear slightly scruffy. My hair is curly and unkempt, like a mad professor. I stood behind the perfectionist, as if photo-bombing him. I took one look at my bird's nest, moved a hand as if to touch it, paused, and said: "No need. Looking good."
The perfectionist did a double-take, then moved on to smoothing his eyebrows.

NOT BEER GARDENS BUT BIERGÄRTEN

7

THERE IS SOMETHING quintessentially British about pub gardens, but it was originally a German invention.

To shade the beer cellars in summer, the Bavarian brewers planted chestnut trees. They also added simple tables and benches, and these areas became known as Biergärten. Naturally, people congregated and socialised. The brewers seized the opportunity and started selling food. Smaller brewers struggled to compete, so complained to King Maximillian, who decreed that only beer and bread was to be served and sold. You could, however, bring your own food. Even today, there are some breweries where this still applies. So if you get caught with your own grub outside a Bavarian brew pub, just claim 'Biergärten Rules'.

Health Benefits

Whiling away the afternoon in a good pub garden is one of life's pleasure. A lunchtime pint feels healthier with a shot of Vitamin D. When surrounded by nature, your soul is being nourished, while your thirst is quenched, so why not treat yourself to another pint? Besides, a sun-drenched pint always tastes delicious.

Gas Burners

These days, with gas burners, you can sit outside until late in the evening too. I was recently in a pub where the gas burner was on a timer switch. This is fine and environmentally friendly, but the timer was too short. Leo and I had to keep pressing the button every few minutes to restart it. It reminded me of those button-operated showers at municipal swimming pools.

Garden Furniture

Most UK pub gardens have the same wooden picnic tables. They are designed to fit four. You can squeeze in six, if you straddle the struts on the end. I'm a straddler.

I am sure whoever owns the rights to this design is worth a fortune. Why are there not more innovative designs? Surely, Ikea could do a pub range – a picnic table which transforms or 'futon-ises' into a shared sunbed.

A wooden lazy boy chair, like the ones Chandler and Joey enjoyed on the sitcom *Friends*, would be idyllic. Imagine being able to enjoy such features as a reclining back, leg rest, cup holder and a retractable tray table.

"How YOU doing?"

Umbrella shades, or parasols, are imperative on a hot day. It helps if they hoist with ease and hold fast. I have felt their wrath before. There is nothing worse than being squashed and trapped underneath, like a fly in a Venus fly trap.

On the first day of summer, pub gardens often contribute to some wonderful comedy tan lines. I was in a pub last year, at the end of a hot day, and there was a couple sat near me with some unfortunate sunburn. The guy had red legs, with a white tan line above the ankle, where his socks had been. That was nothing. His girlfriend had pale legs, with one red triangle. She must have been in total shade, bar a chink of light in the awning. Either that, or she was a fan of Bass.

Insects

The menace of the pub garden is the unwelcome wasp. There is nothing more English than someone flapping and swatting at a picnic table, as if they were on fire.

I used to work at a pub in Bristol called The Prince of Wales. We used to put out small glasses of cola and jam, to entrap the buzzy blighters. No opportunity for a Pepsi Challenge here – wasps aren't fussy. If they could speak, their mantra would be:

"Show me the sugar!"

My Dad's Countryside View

I thought I would ask the views of a proprietor of a traditional country pub, my Dad. I interviewed him in situ, under an apple tree, in The Anchor pub garden. Over a couple of pints of Butcombe, he came up with the following five points:

1 "A perfect pub garden is a vast expanse of lawn, so kids and dogs can run about."

2 "Plenty of plants, but out of reach of dogs, cricket balls and footballs. So raised beds and hanging baskets are very important."

3 "Shade is extremely important. People love sitting under the dappled shade of a tree."

4 "The tables should be clean. No bird poo. They should be wiped down regularly."

5 "The big problem with a sandpit is foxes love to urinate in them!"

The last point gave me a shudder. As a kid I spent hours playing in the sandpit, or a puddle of sandy fox wee, as my Dad has revealed.

City Pub Gardens and Outdoor Drinking

Most country pubs are blessed with gardens, but for the last 18 years I have lived in London, where pub gardens are few and far between. Instead, on warm nights, people crowd outside pubs, chattering on the pavement.

In Mediterranean countries, you sit outside and hope to catch a waiter's eye. Whereas we stand outside and take turns to duck inside, and emerge clasping a triangle of drinks, with a packet of crisps hanging out of our mouth, like a dog ferrying a bone.

There are a few pub gardens which conveniently back onto parks. So The Windmill in Clapham can boast Clapham Common as an extension of its garden. I recently went to The Sun Inn which has picnic tables on the edge of Barnes Common.

Although technically more of a bar than a pub, rooftop gardens have become a big hit. I used to have an office in Dalston, which was part of the Dalston Roof Park. After work, we would walk across the fire escape and enjoy a pint on the roof, overlooking the whole of East London. It was a beautiful way to enjoy the sunset. DJs would spin vinyl, giving it an almost Balearic vibe.

In Peckham, the 10th floor of a multi-storey car park was transformed into a hip bar, called Frank's Cafe. From here you have a breathtaking view of London, and not just Peckham! Netil360 on top of Netil House, in Hackney, is a similar concept. The Queen of Hoxton is a grungy bar, which boasts a beautifully bedecked rooftop. Christmas 2015 was themed with Grimm Fairy Tales in mind.

One of the best places to drink in Bristol is the patio out the back of The Avon Gorge Hotel. From there you have a beautiful view of the Clifton Suspension Bridge and most of South Bristol. I used to love going there as a youth.

Novel Ideas for a Pub Garden

The Willow Inn, in Bourne, just outside Cambridge, houses a tipi in its garden. It has a firepit in the middle, and sofas surrounding. It's very popular for weddings and birthdays. I was there for a comedy night, but the following week they were advertising for a 'Mad Hatter's Tea Party'.

As a kid, the most exciting event to happen in our pub garden was the arrival of a bouncy castle. It was there for three days, and I practically lived in it. My parents recently hired one for my nephew's eighth birthday. I spent most of the day on it, childminding of course.

After looking at pub locations, the interior and exterior of the perfect pub, I think it is high time for a pint.

BEER, BOTH REAL AND OTHERWISE

8

THE FIRST draft of beer is heavenly after a hard day's graft, and even better after no work at all. Beer is something we look forward to; it tackles your thirst in a way wine and spirits do not. So why not reward yourself with an intriguing ale or craft beer, rather than swilling away at some tasteless beer brand.

The English are by nature a shy, repressed bunch and we do require a pint of beer to fire up the engine, cut loose and have fun. Real ale is best enjoyed in company and, fortunately, you have to go to the pub to get the real deal.

Beer is a thoughtful drink. There is nothing better than arriving at a pub earlier than the allotted time, giving you time for an illicit pint and a bit of idle contemplation. *The Idler* magazine recommends slowing down your lifestyle and not being afraid of a leisurely lunchtime pint in a rural country pub, rather than scrambling to meet unrealistic deadlines. A pub is meant to be a relaxing place, where you can leave your troubles at the door and pause, sip and reflect. With luck you will feel recharged by the time you have to re-enter the real world.

Beer was requested in some guise or another in every one of my 'Perfect Pub' shows. Older folk, usually men, would ask for "good draught beer" and younger people "good craft ales."

Real Beer Is Alive

I was reared on good-quality real ale. The first lesson my father taught me was how to order a decent pint. Real ale is alive, unlike most lager. The same beer can taste very different depending on how well it is kept. For example, if the bartender is reluctant to pull a few pints through at the start of the night, the first pint or two of a beer may have been sitting in the pipe for a while, so may taste a little off or musty. The best-tasting beer will be pulled through regularly. My Dad taught me if you visit a new pub, ask what is the most popular beer that night. Although, do refrain from asking what everyone is else is drinking, as you may incur a round.

My First Real Ale Pub Crawl

A few weeks before my 18th birthday, my Dad took me on a real ale pub crawl around Bristol, to show me what's what and where's where. We kicked off with The Old Duke on King Street, near the Harbourside. We drank a couple of pints of Courage Best while a traditional jazz band, called something gentle like The Frampton Foot Warmers, tinkled and plucked away in the foreground. In the air hung a thick fug of cigarette, cigar and pipe tobacco. It felt like I had entered a parallel universe, or travelled back in time.

Next stop, diagonally across the street, was The Llandogger Trow, a 17th-century alehouse, in a Tudor style, with strong literary connections. It was here that Daniel Defoe met Alexander Selkirk, who he used as the basis for the *Robinson Crusoe* story. More pertinent to my book, this place was Robert Louis Stevenson's inspiration for the Admiral Benbow pub in *Treasure Island*. Not only that, but he reputedly wrote parts of the book here. I'm glad I'm not alone in writing in pubs.

I was in awe. *Treasure Island* was one of my favourite books as a kid and here I was, in its birthplace, supping on a pint of Bass. When I was about eight, one of The Anchor regulars, an old sea dog called Jacko, used to tell me his tales of the sea. He wore a sea captain's hat and a donkey jacket, which made him look a dead ringer for Captain Haddock from the Tintin graphic novels. I used to imagine I was Jim Hawkins and he was Blind Pew.

Incidentally the original landlord of The Llandogger Trow in 1664 was also called Hawkins. Was that coincidence or straight borrowing? Last year I took Leo to this very pub, but unfortunately the Tudor style had been replaced by Gangnam style – 'Yo Ho Ho and a bottle of Desperado'. Still, the local clientele, with their Bristolian burr, mostly sounded like pirates.

My Dad and I exited pub two on the tour and headed for The Naval Volunteer, another Tudor-style pub, dating back to 1665. This was becoming a Tudor pub crawl. By rights we should have drunk Kronenbourg 1664, but my Dad plumped for Wadworth 6X, a hearty West Country brew. Leo and I also revisited this pub last year. It is now a very trendy craft beer tavern, where we drank a cider, imbued with almost hallucinogenic qualities. Our fault entirely; we picked the one with the funny name.

The last stop on the father and son pub crawl was The Newquay Steam Tavern, owned by one of my Dad's friends. It was a loud, proud, American-style bar, with middle-of-the-road rock blasting from a middle-of-the-room jukebox. It was perhaps the first and last time my Dad has bought me a pint of lager on English soil. In our house lager is considered outlawed and drinking it would be akin to taking up smoking. I remember my father referring to lager as "a cluster of dead yeast cells"; real ale by comparison was alive and exciting.

The only lager my Dad used to sell in the pub was Harlech Lager, a Welsh beer and I'm not even sure if the pump worked. In my parents' garage there are a few old lagers gathering dust. My brother-in-law Mat once found some lagers in the fridge and wondered whether it was a trick, so plumped for a can of Bass instead.

My Dad and I left The Newquay Steam Tavern after one unfinished pint of lager. After all, it was a school night and tomorrow heralded double geography; a few more pints and I would have been truly glaciated.

My First Forays into Drinking Beer

As a teenager, I was a gawky little cherub and was often asked to produce ID. In fact the last time I was asked for proof of age was while shopping in Lidl, and I was 41. Admittedly, I was buying three litres of cider and some Munch Bunch yoghurt.

Even as a young'un I enjoyed an old-man ale, which helped when attempting to order beer under age. I may have had the face of a baby, but my tastebuds were positively septuagenarian. So I used to drink whatever ale was on tap which, in Bristol back in the early-'90s, included Theakston's, Courage, Butcombe, Bass, Brains, Ruddles, Wadworth 6X, and Smiles.

The only beer I struggled with was Boddingtons. I remember drinking it with my mates, Si and Steve, from the village. Widgets were all the rage back then and the Boddingtons widget was meant to give it a smooth, creamy flow. Or rather, in our case, to froth up like a home-made milkshake. It was undrinkable, so we tried to ladle the froth out with a dessert spoon. In the end we settled on straws; the only one to hand was a curly Krazy straw. Imagine trying to take that to the pub – what clowns we were.

Around this time – the early- to mid-'90s – Jack Dee was the face of John Smith's and was frequently heard wittering about widgets. The widget injected a jet of nitrogen into the beer, hence the name nitro beers. They were marketed with buzz-words like 'smooth' and 'cream flow'. The Irish beer, Caffreys, another creamy beer, was also popular, very drinkable and quite strong. I recall that in the summer of Euro '96 and the height of so-called lad culture, Carling Premier, a cream flow lager, competed to be the drink of the summer. It was first introduced in 1992 to celebrate Carling's sponsorship of the FA Premier League. In my humble opinion, it was completely tasteless, the nearest thing to alcoholic water, and not even hard water.

When I attended Swansea University, aged 19, I was amazed to find folk that hadn't really drunk booze before. Being weaned on beer meant that alcohol was the norm and nothing to go crazy for. I remember watching a football match in the Union bar and one of the guys I was drinking with said:

"Get me a pint in anyway, I'll catch up when I lose the taste."

I was gobsmacked. This was such an alien concept to me, drinking a drink you don't like just to get drunk. I felt like Wychwood Brewery's impish Hobgoblin:

"What's the matter Lagerboy?
Afraid you might taste something?"

Why not pick something you do like? My mistake of course was drinking with Carling Premier's target market, footy lads without a functioning tastebud between them.

We had two student bars on campus, JCs and Divas. I was a Diva, naturally. It's incredible to recall the bar prices. Heineken and Whitbread were a £1 a pint, or you could really push the boat out and plump for a Coors for £1.20, but hardly anyone was that flush. I drank Whitbread in those heady days.

There was also a pub in the town centre called Quids Inn, a pound shop for booze, which made Wetherspoon's seem like Monte Carlo. It was an incredible scene to behold, a public place where you could drink like a student without doing any of the necessary work; sounds like your average arts degree. I should know, I majored in ale appreciation and minored in English literature.

Working in a Brewery

As a student in the mid-'90s I worked in the summer holidays at Smiles Brewery, in Bristol. It was a great place to work. The story goes that the former owner, Ian Williams, had liked the beer so much, he bought the company! As a naive 19 year old my first task was to help organise a charity 'piss up in a brewery'. I'm not saying I couldn't organise a piss up in a brewery, but with all the health and safety regulations it was a lot harder than you might imagine.

Physically, working at Smiles was the hardest job I've ever had. I was an emaciated youth; imagine Mr Muscle with a Where's Wally? haircut. After a month humping barrels – sorry lifting, plonking and shoving – I was almost able to fill out a medium T-shirt.

There were some great characters working at Smiles. The other two warehouse guys were Little Alex and Mexican Alex. It tickles me when a name is popular in a workplace. Before this job I worked in an Asda warehouse with three guys called Gary. They were known as Gary, Gaz and Ga. A fourth would presumably be called G, and a fifth would be called nothing at all. If it was a more middle-class warehouse maybe Garfield would have entered proceedings. But surely he would be headhunted by Waitrose. I digress.

The rules of the brewery were simple: turn up hungover and you have to down a pint. This sounds reasonable until you factor in that we started work at 7.30am. Mexican Alex was regularly penalised, so much so you could add it to his morning routine. Wake up, shower, walk to work, shrug an apology, neck a pint and then kick on with work. I had a cracking summer there. The highlight was signing off a brew, which meant initialling the barrel once it was ready to drink. I thought nothing of it at the time, chalking my initials late one Thursday. However, on the following Friday, during after-work drinks, I had to stand up and taste the first pint as if my reputation were staked on it. A pint of JD 17/07/92. Fortunately it tasted good enough to down, which of course was my colleagues' intention. Turns out this is not actually a thing, I was just the young buck to fall for it.

Real Ale in the Noughties

Real ale wasn't that fashionable in the early-Noughties. Most young folk were drawn to lager. I remember trawling five pubs in Leeds with a comedian friend, Bennet Arron, before we found some good real ale. We joked it would have been easier to buy a gun. Back then, there was often only one real ale on offer in pubs, and even that was gathering dust.

Comedians and journalists often poked fun at the real ale crowd. Looking back on it, even I was a bit dismissive. I found a blog I wrote, in August 2006, after visiting the Great British Beer Festival, in London. I published it on Myspace, which certainly dates it. Reading it back is a trifle embarrassing, and it was only a bit of fun, but I reprint it in its entirety, as a time capsule, to show what people including myself felt about the real ale scene:

> 'I went to the Great British Beer Festival at Earls Court. The Real Ale crowd are a funny looking bunch. It was like drinking in Middle Earth. There were beards aplenty. There seem to be three stages of beard: Geography teacher, Roadie, and Druid. My co-drinker, Dominic Frisby, is three weeks from Druid. The most seasoned real ale drinkers all sported a full beard, huge belly and a red bulb of a nose. Giving the effect of a rather ugly, off-duty Father Christmas.
>
> CAMRA coined the term Real Ale in 1972. The difference between real ale and normal keg beer is, instead of being pasteurised, it has a slow secondary fermentation in the cask to produce a gentle carbonation in the beer. Although delicious, it can react with your tummy.

If you go to a beer festival, arrive early before the farting starts. By 9pm, a cloud of bum fog had descended and engulfed Earls Court, so thick that a pint of Old Jock Strap smelt delightful in comparison.

There were some magnificent names on display.

Some saucy: Village Bike, Bumblehole, and Gobble.

The occasional clever word play or predictive text errors: Fursty Ferret, Ambeardextrous, and Cereal Thriller.

For the upper classes: O Sir, Oscar Wilde Mild, Old Thumper, Top Totty, and Vickys Platonic Tonic

Finally the plain weird: Boondoggle, Waggledance, Old Moggie, Hadda Head Banger, and Chocolate Nutter.

By the end of the day I was a Fursty Ferret, who Boondoggled through the front door and tried to Waggledance for my girlfriend. She Hadda Head Banger, gave me Platonic Tonic and sent me spiralling towards the bathroom to scrub my Bumblehole."

A Beer Revolution is Brewing

A couple of years later, while working in Leeds again, the actor Michael Smiley, a man with his finger on the pulse, took me and another comic, Rich Wilson, to the North Bar. It was the first time a bartender had asked me what kind of drink I was after, before recommending a brew. It was like being served by a beer sommelier. The North Bar blew my mind. There were cool young folk, passionate about real ale, and drinking it in a funky bar, right in the city centre.

There were changes afoot, a beer revolution was brewing, and by the mid-Noughties real ale started becoming fashionable and fun again: Madonna declared her favourite beer was Timothy Taylor on the Jonathan Ross show; her then husband, Guy Ritchie, owned the Punchbowl in Mayfair; Neil Morrissey and Richard Fox also bought a pub and tried to brew their own beer, albeit as part of a TV programme. The point is, real ale ceased to be marginalised and had re-entered the mainstream.

I first noticed this change in the way people perceived beer at a music festival, in 2008. I was performing at End of the Road, at Larmer Tree Gardens, near Salisbury, where I spotted a huge queue for the real ale tent. This festival shunned corporate sponsorship, which is radical as most music festivals struggle without it. For example, Carling sponsors Reading and Leeds, Tennent's Lager is the main sponsor of T in the Park, and Latitude is heavily sponsored by Carlsberg.

By eschewing sponsorship from a corporate brewer, End of the Road were able to attract an eclectic range of intriguing beers like Boondoggle and Burning Gold. Jars of ale were being savoured, slurped, and gulped by a raft of young bohemians and musos sporting beards, bobbly sweaters and flat hats. Ironically, this new breed looked like the real ale enthusiasts of old. How did this change come about? My guess is folk were no longer happy with the mainstream and were instead seduced by cider, the hoppy charms of real ale and the buxom bosom of microbrews.

The recession has led to a reaction against mass-produced corporate products. According to the latest edition of the *Good Beer Guide* 18 pubs are closing per week, but those selling good-quality craft beer are thriving. What does that tell you? Tastes are changing, and maybe you have to adapt to survive. People want a return to independent products lovingly crafted. We want quality for our money, and good real ale and other craft beer straight from the tap is a joy to behold. These days there are more and more try-before-you-buy offers in pubs, which encourages us to experiment with our choices.

The Draught Beer Revolution

The craft beer revolution isn't the first beer revolution. The first hurdle facing my Dad when he bought his pub was in persuading the customers to drink the right beer. In 1969 people drank keg and bottled beer, both plain tasting. For a splash of excitement, they might mix a bottle of stout with a bottle of mild bitter, which was called a black and tan. The problem was you could drink bottles of beer anywhere, but if you wanted a particular real ale you could only buy it in a pub, preferably his pub. So he rolled out barrels of a real ale called Worthington E. How did it go down? My Dad recalls:

> *"The locals avoided it at first, but they were gradually won over. The captain of the rugby team was always asking for a late drink. So I'd simply say, the bar is open, but only if you drink Worthington E. After a while he began to like it, and he and his teammates drank nothing else."*

In fact, when I was born there was a sweepstake for what my name would be. The favourite at 3-1 was Worthington. Even today, some of the old regulars still refer to me as Lord Worthington.

When CAMRA was formed a few years later, in 1972, they were unable to hold rugby players to ransom to preserve draught beer, so opted for campaigning and educating instead.

These days the battle is persuading people to spend their hard-earned cash on a pint in a pub, when you can buy three decent craft beers in the supermarket for the same price.

Tax Breaks for Craft Brewers

Perhaps the turning point for the craft beer revolution was 2002, when our chancellor, Gordon Brown, introduced a Progressive Beer Duty, which gave tax breaks to brewers below a certain size. Suddenly, becoming a small brewer was more commercially viable. From here, the number of small brewers in the UK began to escalate. Initially, brewers still concentrated on draught beer, but many soon adopted the American pale ale style, made famous by Sierra Nevada and its ilk. BrewDog's Punk IPA is a perfect name, as it encapsulates the DIY movement. It can be a short step from home brewing to professional brewing these days.

The craft beer movement has had a profound effect on pubs. Craft beer companies open their own pop-up pubs or shops, to sell direct the customer. My local, the Brockley Brewery, opens its doors every Friday and Saturday, and has a little bar where you can drink in or buy take-outs.

How Do You Define Craft Beer?

'Craft beer' has become a real buzz term in recent years, but what does it actually mean? Around 2012 I defined it as beer made lovingly from a small brewery. It had an independent quality to it. In music terms, it was like a cool indie band.

'Craft beer' has now become a mainstream term. Pubs and supermarkets both advertise that they are selling it. Danny the drug dealer, in the film 'Withnail and I', famously said:

> *"They're selling hippie wigs in Woolworth's, man.*
> *The greatest decade in the history of mankind is over."*

Similarly, when mainstream lager brands use the word 'craft', it has lost its cutting edge. In a television advert, in 2017, Fosters claims to be 'crafted for the thirstiest men on earth.' Is craft beer now nothing more than a fashionable marketing term?

Those who mistrust craft beer claim it is too expensive, too gassy and is served too cold, and they consider it just a pretentious drink for hipsters. Unfortunately, expense is one downside. Producing beer in smaller quantities and often using indulgent lists of ingredients will make it dearer. Even in the supermarkets you have to pay a premium.

While driving back from a gig in Bristol, in September 2018, I listened to a great podcast, the 'Beer o'Clock Show'. They asked listeners to tweet their craft beer definitions. They had over 600 replies and no one could pin down a precise current definition, so even beer aficionados are struggling to articulate exactly what the term means.

CAMRA set about defining real ale from the start. On their website, they describe it thus:

> *'Real ale is a beer brewed from traditional ingredients (malted barley, hops water and yeast), matured by secondary fermentation in the container from which it is dispensed, and served without the use of extraneous carbon dioxide.*
>
> *Brewers use ingredients which are fresh and natural, resulting in a drink which tastes natural and full of flavour. It is literally living as it continues to ferment in the cask in your local pub, developing its flavour as it matures ready to be poured into your glass.*
>
> *Real ale is also known as 'cask-conditioned beer', 'real cask ale', real beer' and 'naturally conditioned beer.'*

What about bottle-produced beers? CAMRA says:

> *'Real ale comes in bottles too! It is a beer that continues to ferment, mature and condition within the bottle. It contains a visible amount of viable yeast cells together with sufficient sugars for fermentation to take place. Bottle-conditioned beers will continue to improve and mature in the bottle but they should be kept in the cool and the dark.'*

CAMRA's take on the whole confusing craft beer issue is that 'all real ale is craft beer, but not all craft beer is real ale.' Wow! We are entering the realms of philosophy. So you could say that real ale is a distinctive, definable part of the craft beer movement. Despite fads and fashions, real ale is still as relevant as ever.

The word artisan refers to someone who crafts an object by hand. I originally thought that craft beer was brewed on a smaller scale than a mainstream brewer, by a skilled artisan.

Then on a tour of Oakham Ales, I discovered they make both real ale and craft beer. The beer is brewed directly above their Grainstore pub and sold downstairs. There are three brewers who bounce around the place with childlike enthusiasm. "It's the personal approach" says assistant brewer, Rory, a cheery, shaggy-haired man mountain with a pair of the biggest hands I've seen. He continues:

> "Some of the bigger Brewers don't get their hands dirty, preferring to operate the brewery by computer and striding around the site in white overalls and hard hats. Where's the fun in that? Not a beard, sweaty shirt or green welly in sight?"

I like his ethos, and it just goes to show the size issue is irrelevant.

So, 500 words later and I have returned to my original definition of a small indie brewer, as like an indie band, with DIY ethos. I am sure the debate will rage on.

Whatever the definition, the good news is quality beer is on the rise. According to the *Good Beer Guide*, in 1970 there were just 191 breweries in the UK and by 2018 the figure had risen to more than 2,500. Long may all British breweries continue to flourish.

Craft Beer Rising

In February 2013 I went to Craft Beer Rising, a beer festival with a great name, at the old Truman Brewery, on Brick Lane in East London. It was a different sort of festival, in that there were some men without beards, slightly less flatulence and actual girls there! The food stalls were different too, with gourmet burgers and a Mark Hix fish and chips stall. It was a cracking day out and I tried some delicious beers from brewers such as Beavertown, Weird Beard and a delicious lager from the winery who produce the award-winning Chapel Down sparkling wine.

I was there visiting my mate, Gavin Hogg, who was running the Bath Ales stall. Bath Ales produce a variety of beers, Gem being the biggest seller. Most people would probably describe it as draught, rather than craft, in style, but technically it's still an indie and therefore fitted the craft remit for the organisers. At the stand I spotted a guy with a twinkle in his eye and a huge bristling moustache like the cartoon Pringle model. I thought, I know that face, he was the head brewer at Smiles when I worked there; no wonder I liked Bath Ales.

On visiting the Great British Beer Festival, at Earls Court and then Olympia, for the last few years, I discovered the real ale crowd and the craft beer crew mingling together, and revelling in their passion for good British beer.

The Beer Selection for Our Perfect Pub

So what beers do we want in our perfect pub? Firstly, you could write a huge number of books addressing this question, and the beauty of it is, it would never end. Beer might be the trickiest chapter in this story to write, because the industry is moving so fast. What is current at the time of writing might be passé by the time of reading.

I think our perfect pub should have a range of quality beers at varying strengths, for a reasonable price. Where possible the beers should be served straight from the barrel. It would be preferable to have one beer on tap from a local brewery too. Chris Betts, a cracking Canadian comedian who used to be a barman, always asks: "What's new and brewed within 10 miles of here?" He was very pleased with his hit rate so far.

My list is just a starting point, the tip of the beer-berg, and by no means definitive. I am a beer-drinking enthusiast, rather than an expert. For ease, I have split my first order into simple categories:

Real Ale Session Beers

You need two good session beers on tap. Like a pair of centre backs in football, they have to be strong, ever-present and dependable. My first pick is Timothy Taylor Landlord (4.3% ABV). It is a beautiful golden amber, whose sweetness is balanced with dry hops. I used to drink it regularly at The Canonbury, in Islington, one of Orwell's favourite pubs. According to Timothy Taylor's website:

'It has won more awards than any other beer, winning both CAMRA's Champion Beer of Britain and the Brewing Industry Challenge Cup four times.'

It was first brewed in 1952, so has a long pedigree. It was launched as Competition Ale, and drinkers were encouraged to name the beer. The winning entry of Landlord won £500 which, back then, was a considerable amount of money.

I am also tickled that the brewery still calls itself Timothy, despite the modern mode for abbreviating everything. Besides, Tim Taylor sounds almost like one of The Goodies.

Being a West Country boy, my second choice is St Austell Tribute (4.2% ABV). It is pale amber, almost bronze in colour. It tastes light and hoppy, and its orange and grapefruit flavours mingle well with the biscuit malt. Although, when supping at the bar with your friends, you are more likely to say "Aaaah, that's hit the spot."

So, one from the North and one from the South. There's always been plenty of rivalry between the North and South of England, but to my mind the biggest difference is headspace. Down south they like a flat head on their beer and up north they prefer a frothy head.

Your own choice may vary, depending where in the UK your perfect pub is set. For example, in Sussex there are some real devotees to Harvey's Sussex Best Bitter (4% ABV), but it tends to taste best close to home, so it would only work if your perfect pub resides in Lewes.

Stronger Cask Beers

As I have got older, I prefer a stronger beer. My favourite is Thornbridge Jaipur (5.9% ABV). I remember Oz Clarke raving about this magical beer in the TV programme *Oz & James Drink to Britain* in 2009. It was every bit as good as Oz described. It tasted different to any beer I had drunk before, full bodied, hoppy, with a citrus glow. This American-style IPA was the first of its ilk in the UK, and arguably started the British craft beer movement. The only problem was it was fairly rare to find it on tap down South. I remember spotting it at The Jolly Butcher's on Stoke Newington High Street which, in turn, soon became my favourite pub. No wonder the celebrated beer writer, Pete Brown, is a also a regular.

My second choice is BrewDog Punk IPA (5.6% ABV). Most readers will have probably tried this; it is an easy-drinking IPA. It has a medium thick body, a fruity malty flavour, and an undercurrent of grapefruit and pineapple. For me, it is the malt that gives it such a recognisable and distinctive taste. Interestingly, one of the founders, Martin Dickie, used to work for Thornbridge before launching BrewDog with his partner, James Watt.

Craft Beer Fridge

I remember in the '90s when a beer fridge was small, and was home to a handful of German and Mexican lagers. These days, with the craft beer boom, our fridge needs to be massive. It is no longer tucked behind the bar; the fridge is a big feature. For example, the wonderful Beer Merchant's Tap, in Hackney Wick, has a wall of fridges displaying 600 bottles and cans from around the world. It is like a bookstore of beer.

My perfect craft beer fridge would be the entire stock of my local craft ale bottle shop. So I threw myself on the mercy of the boys at Salthouse Bottles, in Brockley. I asked them which four beers they would pick for their perfect pub, and on their recommendation I tried the following:

I kickstarted my Friday evening with Tegernseer Hell (4.8% ABV), which tastes like a classic German pilsner. I could drink this by the beer stein; it is very light. They say smell is closely connected to memory, and the aroma took me back to the White Trash Bar, on the Schönhauser Allee in Berlin, opposite the English Comedy Club, where I had been performing years ago. I found this beer to be thirst quenching, yet moreish, a delightfully dangerous combination.

Next up was Cloudwater Pilsner (5.2% ABV). This Manchester brewery is red hot at the moment. Their take on a German-style pilsner is music to my tastebuds. The New Zealand hops provide the baseline, from which the refreshing bitterness sings from the glass.

Then Verdant Howl (7.6% ABV). This Falmouth brewery have created something special. However, it was expensive, and I felt guilty spending that much, but part of you wants to know what a £7 can of beer tastes like. But, after one sip, you forget the price. Very hoppy, it is a powerful American-style IPA, with a delicious mouthfeel. It was super juicy and the fruity bitterness was able to cut through the heavy hops. I felt like donning a cowboy shirt and dancing. If you're a business person, perhaps put it on expenses. Also, it cured my toothache, so it was worth it.

Finally, something sweet to finish: Northern Monk Mango Lassi Heathen (7.2% ABV). Another strong American-style IPA with a mango lassi twist. It tastes like drinking an American IPA out of a glass that previously held mango lassi. I loved it. They say never mix your drinks, but these two are worth mixing. If there was ever a beer to try with a curry, this is it. Even, our cat, Pickle, gave it a second sniff.

Lager on Tap

Again, like our session ales, we want a universally liked lager. Pilsner Urquell (4.4% ABV) fits the bill perfectly. This is a classic and made from the same recipe since 1852.

Gluten-Free Beer

Leo has recently gone gluten-free, and consequently we are drawn to pubs serving that style of beer. Her favourite is Estrella's Damm Daura (5.4% ABV). She is not a big beer drinker anyway, so this suits her. BrewDog Vagabond (4.5% ABV) is far tastier, light bodied, with some caramel; you forget you are drinking gluten-free beer. Two that have been recommended to me, although Leo and I have yet to try them, are Bellfield's Lawless Village IPA (4.5% ABV) and Thornbridge Satzuma (4.5% ABV), also an IPA. Thornbridge head brewer, Rob Lovatt, revealed on the *Beer o'Clock Show* podcast that he used malt with low gluten count and used an enzyme to remove the rest. He makes it sound so straightforward, like a scientific magician.

Alcohol-Free Beer

Some people might shudder at the very idea of alcohol-free beer, and consider it a contradiction in terms. However, for the designated driver, or those thirsting for a beer but wishing to give their liver a night off, this may appeal. I quite enjoyed BrewDog Nanny State (0.5% ABV) which, although still quite watery, did have a delicious hoppy taste. Erdinger Weizen Alkoholfrei (0.5% ABV) is a refreshing alternative too. On the same podcast mentioned above, I was also quite intrigued to hear Rob Lovatt informing us that for their alcohol-free beer Beck's would brew as normal, and then use a very expensive machine to remove the alcohol, whereas at Thornbridge they decided to brew their alcohol-free beer from scratch. I must say, if you were a millionaire, you could invest in an alcohol-removing machine; it would be the ideal hangover cure!

AGRICULTURAL CHAMPAGNE

9

I GREW UP IN CIDER COUNTRY. The kids today might be forgiven for thinking that's Ireland, such is the marketing allure of Magners. South-west England and the three counties of Herefordshire, Worcestershire and Gloucestershire are traditionally synonymous with cider.

When I worked behind the bar of The Prince of Wales, in Bristol, one of the regulars used to request "A pint of agricultural please." He delighted in anyone looking quizzical, where upon he would say, "Cider is agricultural champagne."

Fortunately, he stopped short of drinking it in a glass flute, and opted for his own tankard instead. I never asked him whether he also regarded pork scratchings as West Country caviar.

I started stand-up in the South-West and one of my early short routines was:

"I was three years old when I had my first taste of alcohol. I fell in a bucket of rough cider. You know what I mean by rough cider, made locally without instructions! It was so strong, a dog licked me and passed out."

It's fun giving a daft definition of rough cider for an audience, but the truth is not many folk know the difference between real cider and mere cider.

Real Cider

Like real ale, there is cider and real cider. CAMRA defines real cider thus:

> 'Real cider is a long-established traditional drink which is produced naturally from apples and is neither carbonated or pasteurised.'

Wowsers! You only have to think of the amount of fizzy ciders, made from concentrate, to realise how few are actually real cider. CAMRA's definition might seem a trifle harsh, as there are some fantastic traditional and craft ciders which do not fit the criteria, but that does not make them inferior.

UK law defines cider, or unreal cider, as containing at least 35 per cent apple or pear juice, which may be from concentrate. It would be enlightening to find out the actual juice content of a cider, but brands are not bound to declare that figure, and seem reluctant to do so.

You may be curious what the rest – potentially 65 per cent – is made from. According to cider duty rates, approved ingredients allowed in cider include: apple aromas, high fructose corn syrup, fructose and an assortment of colourings and additives. HM Revenue & Customs state:

> 'If your cider or perry contains other ingredients, it's classed as "made-wine" and you'll need to register and submit returns for Wine Duty.'

In this chapter I shall be addressing all manner of ciders, as I would like our pub to be perfect, rather than just purist.

Very Brief History of Cider

Ancient Britons reportedly made their own æppelwīn which, as you might guess, roughly translates as apple wine. It was very bitter, so they added honey as a sweetening agent. Although the Romans were fond of apples, there is no actual evidence of cider making until the arrival of the Normans, who were keen apple growers and cider makers. They brought over their own sweeter apples, the Costard and the Pearmain – a confusing name for an apple, but perfect for cider making. The introduction of these two apples meant honey was no longer needed as a sweetener.

The French word, *cidre*, first appeared in 12th century, from which we derive the word cider. Many of us may have snorted at Stella using the continental name for their cider, but it turns out it was the original term. It is hard work writing *cidre* on a laptop, as my computer keeps trying to auto-correct it to cider!

Cider was often used as a form of payment, and the first written record of this was from a manor in Runham, Norfolk, in 1204.

Monks made cider, alongside wine, in medieval times, and sold it to the public. The Bishop of Bath was said to have bought cider presses for his monastery in 1230. Back then, if you wanted the best booze, you needed to know a monk. The monastery was the unofficial off licence of the day.

"Tonight, we drink, but before we do, we need to call in at the monastery to grab a few gallons."

Medieval farm workers used to worship the apple trees at Yuletide, in a ceremony called wassailing. They would toast the health of the trees, hoping for a good crop the following year. They celebrated by drinking cider, singing, and dancing in the orchards. I think we have all inadvertently wassailed, at some point in our lives. Wassailers would also pour cider on the roots of the tree. Hmm; I draw the line at spillage.

Henry VIII sent Richard Harris, a fruiterer, to France on a fruit-finding expedition. He sourced various new varieties, including the pippin, and established orchards in Kent.

During the 18th century there was a real focus on planting

cider apples in Herefordshire, Gloucestershire, Somerset and Devon. Different varieties of cider apple were planted, with delicious names like Foxwhelp, Meadgate, Eliot and the Irish Cockagee. The famous Kingston Black was the variety which put Somerset on the cider map; and the styre apple was the beast responsible for making rough cider, which sent us a few of us 'styre' crazy.

In the late-19th century cider making was viewed more scientifically. Studies were made to discover the best varieties of cider apple, and optimum production processes. Imagine being the first professor of cider, stumbling around in a white jacket and being greeted with, "Ah, Doctor Cider, I presume." These days, your title would be ciderologist.

Today, many mainstream cider producers import their apple concentrate from the continent. There is, however, nothing better than small cider producers, using their own apples. Like craft beer, craft cider is also on the rise. Organic ciders are also becoming increasingly popular; these are ciders made from apple orchards in which no pesticides have been used.

The Wurzels

The unofficial cider ambassadors are The Wurzels. They're famous for singing about cider and lending combine harvesters, and are to cider what the Beach Boys were to surfing. They've even invented their own style of music, Scrumpy & Western. I was weaned on The Wurzels. We had a cassette recorder and only four tapes; one of them was 'The Very Best of The Wurzels.' I learnt 'The Combine Harvester' song and 'I Am a Cider Drinker' alongside the usual nursery rhymes.

Cider Farms and Cider Making

At my school, cider was even part of the curriculum. I remember visiting Sheppy's Cider Farm, in Somerset, as part of an A-level Geography field trip. Most of us were 17 at the time and all paid particular attention to the tasting tutorial. They say your school days are the happiest days; well, this one certainly was.

As a student, I had a job at Long Ashton Cider, on the outskirts of Bristol. The site had historical significance. In 1903 it was host to the National Fruit and Cider Institute, created to improve the West Country cider industry. It became the Long Ashton Research Station when it amalgamated with Bristol University in 1912. During World War II, when there was a shortage of vitamin C, Long Ashton came up with a solution, and invented Ribena.

While working at Long Ashton, I will never forget the first time I leant over an industrial steel vat of cider. It was quite a shock; the fumes were intoxicating, especially with a nose as big as mine!

One of the bonuses of working at a cider farm was being given a jug of cider to take home. It was a glass jug with a finger handle, a showstopper when taken to parties.

I was only an odd job man, but I learnt a lot on the odd job.

Six Cider Facts

1. Scrumpy is a West Country nickname for cloudy, unfiltered cider. The word comes from scrump, which means a small or withered apple.
2. Ordinary cider, made from concentrate, can be made at any time. But real cider can only be pressed twice a year, May and October, when the fruit is ripe.
3. Cider makers invented *méthode champenoise* a century before Dom Perignon. It is this secondary fermentation which makes cider sparkle with bubbles.
4. Captain Cook carried cider on his ship to treat his crew for scurvy. I currently take vitamin C pills; maybe I should wash them down with a drop of cider.
5. 45 per cent of all UK apples are now used to make cider.

6. There are over 365 cider apple varieties, and each one produces a different flavour, one for each day of the year. I say, an apple a day keeps the ciderologist away.

The website www.real-cider.co.uk tells us:

> *'Cider apples fall into four categories, according to the tannin, sugar and acidity levels:*
> *1. Bittersweets are high in tannin and low in acid – e.g.: Yarlington Mill, Dabinett*
> *2. Sweets are low in both – e.g.: Sweet Coppin, Sweet Alford*
> *3. Bittersharps are high in both – e.g.: Kingston Black, Broxwood, Foxwhelp*
> *4. Sharps are low in tannin and higher in acid – e.g.: Frederick, Crimson King'*

Gabe Cook, an actual ciderologist, explained the different flavours in an interview with the *Independent* in 2013:

> *'Ciders of different apple blends will taste quite different to one another. Some are more acid-forward, some bold, rich and tannic, and others full and fruity. It is the interplay between acidity, tannin and sweetness that makes the great ciders stand out from the also-rans; the supreme from the scrump.'*

Cider in the 1990s

Cider is currently very fashionable, but when I went to uni, in the mid-'90s, the only people I knew who drank cider were goths, 'crusties' and coeliacs. It was a must at the Glastonbury Festival, where Burrow Hill cider, served from the famous cider bus, was the order of the day. Jugs of locally made real cider were also sold at roadsides, all the way down to the festival. Stories of their strengths ranged from strong to hallucinogenic.

For the rest of us, I am ashamed to say, cider was sometimes considered a novelty drink. Twenty years ago my friends and I would decide to seek out a cider pub. Our favourite was

The Coronation Tap, in Bristol. It is a Georgian pub in the cobbled back streets of Clifton, nestled near the Suspension Bridge. The cider is served straight from the barrel and so strong that drinking in half pints is recommended. Their top seller is Exhibition, made by Thatchers, and is a hefty 8.5% ABV. The other good advice I received was to never sit down when drinking strong cider, as you might struggle to get back up. One cider that tickled my fancy back then was called Legbender. It did exactly what it said on the tin.

Aikido Jim and 'Withnail and I'

One of my best friends at university was Aikido Jim. There was a bountiful supply of James's, so we all had a nickname. Jim was known as Aikido because he thought about doing aikido; he never actually did it, but talked about the possibility. I was known as Louie, a name I made up on the spot. (My uni friends still call me Louie today.)

Aikido Jim was worried he might be an alcoholic, so I took him to AA and waited outside during the meeting. After-wards, our task was to do something non-alcohol related. We settled on a trip to the cinema. What could possibly go wrong? There was only one film showing on campus: *Withnail and I* – a movie celebrating drunken exploits. For those unlucky few who have yet to see the film, it is the hilarious story of two struggling actors, played by Richard E. Grant and Paul McGann, who seek solace in booze and go on holiday by mistake. Within minutes of the film finishing, Aikido was at the bar ordering the film's signature booze combo:

> *"Two large gins, two pints of cider. Ice in the cider."*

Sober mission aborted.

I would often order that round for my friend Simon Shaw (not the rugby player). We referred to it as a Withnail.

Don't worry, Aikido Jim was never properly diagnosed as

an alcoholic, just a bit over-zealous at the bar occasionally. He currently lives with his family in New Zealand. He is still yet to do aikido, but the nickname lives on.

I am an avid *Withnail and I* fan. Here's a picture of me as a fanboy, having my photo taken with poor Paul McGann, who is probably exhausted from fans yelling quotes from the film all the time.

I do wonder whether it was a *Withnail and I* fan who started the trend of cider with ice? The film came out in 1986 but had a cult status on VHS for years after.

Cider with Ice

Magners seemed to explode in the summer of 2012. (Incidentally, Magners was the name given to Bulmers cider sold outside Ireland.) It was a huge marketing triumph, especially in choosing to sell the cider in bottles, which meant you could load your pint glass with ice without skimping on any precious cider.

Fruit-Flavoured Ciders

The next wave was the fruit ciders. Kopparberg cider, from Sweden, was the first I became aware of. It had two flavour options: pear and summer fruits. A few of my friends loved it, but the only place I knew to buy it was a certain Swedish furniture outlet. Suddenly, meatballs and Billy bookcases were not the only reason to visit Ikea, and Kopparberg was flying out of their self-assembly shelves. Fortunately, you didn't have to make it yourself. It was however quite surreal, scrambling over futons to find cider; like an alcohol assault course.

Kopparberg cider was launched in 1994 and is now the best-selling pear cider in the world. Another Swedish cider, Rekorderlig, followed in 1996. The New Zealand cider, Old Mount, was established in 1947, and began experimenting with fruit flavours in 2008. Heineken have since imported Old Mount to the UK and made it part of their portfolio.

I imagine hardcore real cider fans bristling at the mere thought of flavoured fruit cider and wincing at the mention of pear cider, rather than its original term, perry.

Perry

Perry is made from fermented perry pears, which are grown especially for perry production, using the same method as for cider.

You don't often see it being sold in pubs, for the reason that the production volumes are so small. When I worked at Long Ashton Cider we only shifted a few cases of perry a week. It is revered among the Three Counties and Welsh Borders, so there is a thirst for it. The problem is there aren't enough quality perry pears grown to satisfy demand. Although the perry tree can bear fruit after three years, it takes 30 years to reach maturity. This requires patience, a quality sadly lacking in today's fast-moving markets.

CAMRA supports perry by showcasing it at its beer festivals and even runs a competition to determine the best perry, with gold, silver and bronze awards.

The first mass market perry was Babycham. There was a famous advert, set in a club, where a gentleman asks a girl whether she would like a drink; she replies, "I'd love a Babycham." The music stops and everyone freezes. The crowd parts, and a dude in a leather jacket and sunglasses demands, in a very deep voice, "Hey... I'd love a Babycham," giving it the seal of approval. The advert was screened in 1986; I was 12 at the time, but it is still burned into my memory. Maybe it was screened during the Mexico World Cup? Unfortunately the image of Babycham and its competitor, Lambrini, probably didn't do traditional perry makers any favours.

Cider Advertising and I

In 2012 Carlsberg launched Somersby Cider for the UK market. I have to confess I had a small part in the Somersby TV advert, which came out in 2013. The concept was a play on the word apple. It spoofed an 'Apple style' shop launch and viewed Somersby cider like an Apple product. It was called 'The Somersby Store', and is available to watch online.

In the audition we were encouraged to riff on connections between cider and technology. Growing up as I did in the West Country, and having a geeky look, I was in my element, and ended up contributing a few lines to the advert.

It was filmed in Argentina, because it was one of the cheapest places to film, with guaranteed sunshine, in February. Argentina was beautiful. We were lucky enough to stay in Palermo, which is a very cool part of Buenos Aires. When the shoot was finished, we were not offered any Somersby to toast with, so we drank a few Quilmes and Malbecs instead.

I have since tasted Somersby with one of my co-actors, David Ahmad, and it is a fairly standard cider from concentrate. It is perhaps telling that the marketing people decided to align themselves with a trendy technological product, rather than a fresh apple. It often features at music and arts festivals like Latitude, where Carlsberg supply it, alongside Tuborg.

Hot and Spicy Cider

Talking of music festivals, the End of the Road Festival, situated in Larmer Tree Gardens, near Salisbury, introduced me to hot cider. Every year there is the familiar blue West Country cider bus parked amongst the catering stalls, the main attraction of which is hot and spicy cider. The vendors warm cider in a cauldron and add cloves. On a cold night it is divine and warms your cockles. Beware of its subtle strength; you can feel like someone is wrapping you in a warm blanket, while gently punching you in the head!

It is said Kentish cider mills were noted for producing strong spiced cider during the reign of Henry II. With their sculpted beards, and fancy clothes, maybe the Plantagenets were the original hipsters.

Cider Pubs

There are some incredible cider pubs in the UK. I mentioned the Coronation Tap earlier, but Bristol now also boasts The Apple. This a beautiful floating Dutch barge, moored in the centre of Bristol, at the south end of King Street. They offer a range of over 40 cider-related drinks, including their own, the Old Bristolian, usually sold in half pints, as it is 8.4% ABV.

The Cider Tap, directly opposite the Euston Tap, outside Euston station, is a cracking cubbyhole of a pub. The last time I went there was to send off my old friend Simon Shaw, who was joining the New Zealand air force. After a few hours supping cider, we were all flying that night.

There are other notorious cider pubs I have read about, but yet to visit, including The Cider House, in Defford, Worcestershire, and Ye Old Cider Bar in Newton Abbot, Devon.

To help identify a good cider pub, CAMRA has initiated a badge scheme, where they distribute 'Real Cider Sold Here' window stickers to pubs who regularly sell real cider. They are a kite mark for cider.

Which Ciders to Stock

Deciding which ciders to stock may depend on the location of our perfect pub. If it is situated in a traditional cider area, we may need to triple our orders.

I would like to see at least one real cider on tap. My weapon of choice would be Westons Old Rosie. It is easy drinking and delicious. Although cloudy, it is still light, crispy and dry, and comes in at 7.3% ABV.

Not all real cider is available on draught, but it would be fun to serve the occasional cider from a box or vat, as if bought at the farm gate. This way we could delve into the likes of Burrow Hill and Wilkins cider, both from Somerset.

Of the mainstream brands, I would plump for Thatchers Gold. It's a refreshing, medium dry, session cider at 4.8% ABV. A good alternative would be Aspall's, from Suffolk, also medium dry, and, according to Aspall's, it goes well with a mild curry. Kingfisher and Cobra – beware!

Behind the bar should be a fridge stocking a veritable feast of bottled cider, spanning real, traditional, and craft. Leo and I are quite partial to Henry Westons Vintage Cider. It's medium dry and oak aged, which gives it a real smoothness. I have to say it is a regular in our fridge at home, and dangerously drinkable at 8.2% ABV. If you're looking for something less pokey, then Westons also produce Wyld Wood organic cider. It is also medium dry and a mere 6% ABV.

We would also offer an assortment of fruit ciders, especially in the summer months, and hot spicy cider in winter.

My Cider Summation

There is a whole world of cider to discover. I appreciate my personal recommendations centre around the West Country and the Three Counties, but that is where I grew up and spent my formative cider-drinking years. However, the drink is far more encompassing than a mere farmer's tipple, despite the cries of "Another pint of Agricultural young 'un." Do seek out some real cider, wherever you see the window sticker. Try a real perry too; perry needn't just be an alcopop.

ALL ABOUT STOUT

IN HIS perfect pub essay, George Orwell drooled:

> 'The special pleasure of this lunch is that you can have
> draught stout with it. I doubt whether as many as
> 10 per cent of London pubs serve draught stout,
> but the Moon Under Water is one of them. It is a soft,
> creamy sort of stout, and it goes better in a pewter pot.'

I can imagine the bar staff whispering:

> "Ere comes that Animal Farmyard fella,
> better dust off a pewter pot for 'im."

I like the fact that Orwell was discerning enough to choose the right receptacle for his stout. It is also interesting to note that in 1946 stout was rare in London pubs. It was, however, just after the war.

Porter

There is no definitive origin for the word porter. The CAMRA website says 'it acquired the name Porter as a result of its popularity among London's street-market workers.' They craved a more nutritious and wholesome beer, as fuel.

Stout Porter

Stout was originally known as stout porter, and the term was used to describe a porter with a higher alcohol percentage. These days porters can be more potent than stouts and vice versa. The two beer styles have blended into one.

Originally, this dry black brew was heavily hopped and made from roasted barley, which gave it such a distinctive taste. Orwell claimed his draught stout was soft and creamy, but the pressurised containers loaded with nitrogen weren't available until the 1960s, so Orwell's stout might have poured using the two-cask system. One cask contained fresh maturing stout and the other a more mature brew. His pewter pot would have been filled with the fresh stout and, when it had settled, would be topped up with the more mature brew. Nowadays the thick creamy head derives from mixing the beer with nitrogen and carbon dioxide when poured.

Arthur Guinness

Ireland is synonymous with stout, but the style was actually based on English porter, which was imported or 'im-portered' to Ireland in the 18th century. Dublin water, like London water, is perfect for making dark beer. The founder of Guinness was Arthur Guinness. I like to imagine the reason he didn't use his full name was that Arthur Guinness sounds too much like 'Half a Guinness,' and sipping halves is bad for business.

Arthur Guinness initially brewed ale, but was so wowed by the porter shipped over from England that by 1799 he had completely converted to the dark side of the drop and produced nowt but stout.

In the 1820s the second Arthur Guinness (Do they ever learn? Although I suppose two halves does make a pint) perfected an extra stout porter, which simply became known as stout. By this time, Guinness had become the biggest brewer in Ireland. Their St James's Gate brewery resembled a walled city, with its own railway system and even a small power station. His son Benjamin transformed Guinness into a global phenomenon. In 1886 Guinness was floated on the stock exchange as a public company, worth a cool £6 million despite owning no pubs or not spending any money on advertising. The latter would soon change.

Four Types of Guinness

There are four main types of Guinness, although the firm has brewed special blends for various occasions over the years. The strength and style varies depending on the market. The ubiquitous and deliciously creamy Draught Guinness you see in pubs is 4.1% ABV. Guinness Extra Stout is 4.3% ABV and is shipped in the bottle. It is heavy on the hops and uses unmalted roasted barley, to give it a complex bitter flavour. Thirdly, Guinness Foreign Extra, not to be confused with Extra Foreign, for racial reasons, has an astringent kick and weighs in at 7.5% ABV. Finally, the rare Guinness Special Export is a punchy 8% ABV although it actually tastes quite mellow. This is produced exclusively for the Belgian market, where they love a strong brew. In fact the Belgians would probably describe Stella Artois as a gentle drop.

Marketing

Growing up, I remember Guinness being easily the most expensive pint behind the bar. My Dad claimed its price reflected the amount of money spent on advertising. Guinness became known as *the* Irish beer from the early-19th century and its brand was strong from the start. The stencilled label, with the harp emblem, first appeared in 1862 and has remained ever since. The harp harks from the Trinity College motif. Guinness was one of the first beers to earn international recognition. This was born out of necessity, as it had saturated its home market. By its 200th birthday, in 1959, 60 per cent of its production was purely for export.

During a period of market research some folk claimed they felt better after a pint of Guinness. Marketing boffins interpreted that data with one of the most successful-ever marketing slogans:

'Guinness Is Good for You.'

Guinness has always carried the myth that it is healthy, despite containing no more iron than any other beer. Mrs Beeton, the Delia Smith of the 19th century, didn't do the advertising campaign any harm when she advised women to drink stout when pregnant or anaemic. Obviously, I cannot get pregnant, but I am feeling a little wan. Maybe I should self-medicate with a gorgeous Guinness.

Incredibly, before the 1930s, Guinness had no advertising and relied solely on word of mouth. The hardship of the 1930s forced them to rethink with slogans like the one above. S. H. Benson (great name for a secret agent – Shush Benson) was responsible for the copy and John Gilroy drew the cartoons. Among their most successful ads, during their fertile period of the '30s and '40s, were 'Guinness for Strength', 'Lovely Day for a Guinness', and 'Guinness Makes You Strong,' which we have all seen decorating the walls of Irish-theme pubs. They also developed a Toucan obsession. Maybe it was subliminal advertising, telling us to buy two cans instead of one, if you pardon the pun, and allowing you to rectify the damage done by its creator, Mr 'Half a' Guinness.

Pouring Guinness

The double-pour method of Guinness was exemplified with the marketing slogan 'Good things come to those who wait.' Head office bods from Diageo, the company which now owns Guinness, reckon the perfect pouring time is 119 seconds. I cannot imagine those beautifully laid-back folk, from rural Ireland, timing the pour on their wristwatches – or indeed sporting wristwatches. It would interrupt the tranquillity. The fact that 119 seconds is one second under two minutes appeals to me. It shows a similar sense of humour to my Dad, who embraces an odd number and always wishes to meet in the pub at strange times, such as 10.11pm or 9.13pm.

So what is a thirsty Guinness drinker to do, while he waits for his pint to settle, before the second pour? Dance to 'Guaglione' by Perez Prado, was Guinness' answer. 'The Dancing Man,' launched in 1995, was perhaps one of the most iconic adverts of the '90s. The accompanying song went to number one in the pop charts and spawned numerous wacky dances in pubs, clubs and bars.

TV Advertising

Guinness really hit its stride when it came to TV advertising. The first ones I remember were the series of ads, featuring the actor Rutger Hauer, in the late-1980s. In each advert a cool Rutger, dressed all in black, philosophises upon the vagaries of modern life. The lines were delivered with a delicious deadpan wit before sipping a pint of Guinness, like a nightclub comic, dragging on a cigarette, after delivering a killer punchline. In case we were in any doubt, 'Pure Genius' is stamped on the screen. No mention of the product, just the attitude. The real genius was in the advertising.

All the scripts were razor sharp and the visuals beautifully shot. My particular favourite was a serious Rutger claiming he is accused of taking himself too seriously. Cue Hauer leaning into his Guinness and coating his nose with cream. "Not guilty" he chimes. Quite literally the face of Guinness. By the end of his stint his immaculate blonde locks had turned white, and with his black clothes, he began to actually look like a pint of Guinness. During his stout reign, Rutger embodied the philosophy of the perfect pint of Guinness. He covered most subjects apart from hitchhiking, thankfully, because he has had previous.

Draught Guinness in a Can

In 1989 draught Guinness was launched, or rather compressed, into a can. It did so with the aid of a genius invention, the widget. A widget is not only a great name for a dog, but is also a small round ball which injects nitrogen into the beer. Guinness contains more nitrogen than carbon dioxide, and this prevents the beer from being fizzy. As the ring pull is cracked open, the widget surges the can with nitrogen and provides that rich, creamy head we hold so dear.

Pouring Guinness with 'The Surge'

In 2006, Guinness followed up with a new method of serving beer called 'The Surge'. The barkeep pours the beer from a can into a glass, places the glass on a plate, and presses a button which surges ultrasonic shockwaves through a pint of Guinness, which gives it the surge and settle effect. While I half admire the science, it destroys the romance and tradition of pouring a pint of Guinness. This is less about thinking outside the box, and more about microwaving outside the oven.

Black Lager

I read in March 2010 Guinness began experimenting with a black lager. My Dad tried to market a black lager, in the late-1990s, during the bottled-beer trend. It was called Hippo. The bottle was black with a picture of a black hippo. As you drank, the bottle became clear to reveal the hippo. At the time I thought it was neat. Maybe my Dad was a little ahead of his time. Good things come to those who... hang on.

Three Guinness Facts to Tickle Your Friends with:

1. Although Guinness is depicted as black in its advertising, it is actually a dark shade of ruby.
2. Despite its reputation as a 'meal in a glass', Guinness only contains 198 calories in a pint. That is less than in the equivalent amount of skimmed milk or orange juice.

3 Brewers state that normal draught Guinness should be served at 6 degrees Celsius and Extra Cold at 3.5 degrees Celsius. I drive a Volkswagen Golf and the dashboard gives me a warning sign at 4 degrees. The next time it hits 3.5 I shall declare it Extra Cold, not with the Wind Chill Factor, but with the added Guinness factor.

Drinking Guinness in Ireland

People often say that Guinness tastes better in Ireland, but is this fact or fiction? Some say it's the Dublin water that makes the difference. The Guinness brewery at St James's Gate is in the heart of Dublin, which overlooks the River Liffey. However, the brewers don't use the water from the Liffey. The actual water they use is from a spring up in the Irish mountains.

In the late-1990s I went travelling around Ireland with my friend, Jon Dyke. We arrived on a car ferry from Fishguard and docked at Wexford. Our first port of call was a pub called O'Looney's. It was as mad as it sounds. We arrived late after-noon and sunlight was streaming through the windows. The harsh glare obscured the horse racing on TV, rendering every finish a photo-finish. There was a handful of drinkers sitting at the bar. The first thing I noticed was the level of the drinks; they were either full or almost empty, never in-between. After a while, my friend Jon noticed there seemed to be a local method to drinking Guinness.

How to Drink Like a Local in Ireland:

1 Order your Guinness
2 When it arrives, ignore it for five minutes. Sorry, 300 seconds.
3 Once your pint has settled, attack it.
4 Wink at bartender for the next one and repeat to fade.

I say attack, whereas my friend Jon would say "You take a big bite." He reckons a pint of Guinness is about six bites.

We definitely felt the Guinness tasted smoother in Dublin, than say Bristol. Was this true or were we swept away in the moment? The French wine industry has a word called *terroir*, which is hard to pinpoint, but roughly means that a wine you drink in France encompasses not only the taste, but the vibe, the surrounding countryside, the weather, the atmosphere and the overall conditions in which it was conceived. Terroir could be described as a wine's DNA. Similarly, is drinking a Guinness in Ireland better because of the Irish terroir or 'the craic'?

It was a delightful evening. We ate so much Guinness we forgot to have dinner and still we wanted more. I remember saying to the landlord:

> *"When does this bar close?"*
> *"Ahhh... October!" came the perfect reply.*

We awoke next day in a day-glo tent. The sun was beating down; hang on, this is Ireland, the sun was tickling the flanks of our tent. We began a ritual that would last all holiday:

> *"Are you awake?"*
> *"Yes."*
> *"Have you moved your head?"*
> *"I daren't risk it."*
> *"I'll go first."*
> *"Are you ok?"*
> *"I'm fine. Now I'm gonna attempt to stand. Still fine. My Gawd this Guinness is good. Double figures and no hangover.*
> *I'm ready for a breakfast pint."*
> *"Me too."*

Gin-ness

Around that time my friend Simon Shaw and I were asked to guard a marquee overnight. All we had to do was to sleep over and protect it from being damaged. We invited a few friends over for drinks. Unfortunately, during the evening Simon split up with his girlfriend and was feeling despondent. I summoned all the remnants of our supplies: one bottle of gin and four cans of Guinness. In the heat of the moment I invented a new drink – 'Ginness.' They say 'There's no I in team'; well, there's nothing left of U in 'Ginness'. You *will* be broken. It is like trying to put unleaded petrol in a diesel truck. After which, the only vehicle you are capable of driving is a porcelain one.

Other Irish Stouts

Of course there are other stouts than Guinness. In the early-19th century Beamish was the biggest brewer of stout in the land, even bigger than Guinness. Unfortunately, by the mid-20th century, this Cork based brewery had gone to rack and ruin. Fortunately, a succession of foreign owners have enabled it to keep brewing and you still see it in most Irish pubs.

Murphy's was also established in Cork, in 1856, by the Murphy brothers. It ran into financial trouble in the 1960s after an ill-fated deal, with Watneys, to sell Red Barrel throughout Ireland. The government had to rescue the brewery, but it survived and was finally bought by Heineken in 1983. Since then, its business has boomed and you can buy Murphy's worldwide.

Oyster Stout has become popular in recent years. It is 4.8% ABV and brewed at the Porter House in Dublin. Its name derives from the recipe, which includes real oysters in the brew. They say champagne and oysters is the way to a person's heart, so surely Oyster Stout would make the perfect Black Velvet cocktail. This stout-tail is a mix of equal parts champagne and stout, but how was it invented? Was someone double-parked on a pint of Guinness and a glass of Bollinger and thought: "Ah well, I'll just tip it in."

The real story originates from the Brooks's Club in London in 1861. A bartender created the drink to commemorate the passing of Prince Albert. The drink was supposed to symbolise the black clothes worn by the mourners. Of course the cocktail couldn't be called a Prince Albert, because that refers to a very different tail.

Intriguingly, stout and champagne are very different densities, so form two separate layers when mixed. To achieve this neatly, the champagne is poured as usual and then the stout is poured over the reverse side of a spoon, so the stout cascades gently over the champagne. If you use cider in place of champagne, it is usually called a 'Poor Man's Black Velvet,' but who would order a drink with such negative connotations? Why not call it a Stout Bubble, a Farmers' Fetish or even a PM's Black Velvet? Lastly on the subject, I am informed with a cider B.V. the stout is poured first. If the cider is first into the glass, it is called a Black Adder. I imagine if you find a turnip in your glass, it would be called a 'Baldrick'. Clear as stout?

What Stouts Would We Stock in Our Perfect Pub?

Guinness would definitely feature in our perfect pub; however, I would insist on serving it from a traditional beer fount, rather than a surge mechanism. We may also serve Extra Cold during the summer months.

The Resurgence of London Porters

In the aftermath of World War II the rationing of roasted barley in Britain affected the volume of beer production. Stout, with its celebrated reputation for being healthy and nutritious, thanks to Guinness, had become fashionable and poured across the Irish Sea. London Porter was left behind. It was not until the recent microbrewery boom that porter re-emerged from the shadows as an exciting drink. Now most craft brewers pride themselves on their porter, as well as their IPAs.

I only started drinking porters around five or six years ago. They are a delicious winter warmer on a bracing November night. With notes of coffee, nuts, chocolate and toffee, a few porters can taste like Christmas in a glass. In summer, a chilled porter is a refreshing twist on traditional drinking. Most recently, my publisher, Simon Hall, introduced me to the civilised concept of finishing a evening's drinking with a half pint of stout, or porter. At last orders, it is certainly more healthy than a round of whisky.

At the Great British Beer Festival 2017, Daniel Neilson, author of CAMRA's *Wild Pub Walks*, introduced me to a mind-blowing 9% ABV Imperial Stout called Troubadour. The chocolate and toffee made me think of the phrase, pudding beer. A few months later I was gigging down in Eastbourne and Daniel's wife sauntered over to the act's table, presented me with a couple of bottles in a bag, and declared "I hear this is your favourite," and walked off. The other acts were flabbergasted. "Does that happen a lot?" one said.

"Well, beer writing does have its occasional perks."

That's what a cool person would say, and I am not that guy. I believe I muttered something terribly humble, whilst peeking into the brown paper bag, and scanning its contents.

A revolving selection of intriguing stouts and porters would be ideal in our perfect pub. I could compile an extensive list; however, I feel the following would be a reasonable starting point. I must stress, I am an enthusiast, rather an expert, so please feel free to differ.

"Oh I will!" holler the beer anoraks

Five Porters and Stouts to Sample

Railway Porter – The Five Points Brewery Co. 300ml, 4.8% ABV. This is a delightfully rich London Porter, with notes of bitter chocolate, roasted coffee, with a hint of caramel. For me, it's a perfect post-dog-walk drop.

Milk Stout – The Bristol Beer Factory. 500ml, 4.5% ABV. This is a deliciously drinkable milk stout. The sweetness of the chocolate is balanced by the bitterness of the coffee. I love its milky smoothness and certainly wouldn't mind a couple of pints delivered to my doorstep each morning.

Millionaire – The Wild Beer Co. 330ml, 4.7% ABV.
What a fun beer! You can really taste the salted caramel, which blends beautifully with the chocolate from Valrhona cocoa nibs. If Guinness is a meal in a glass, this is a pudding in a bottle. In a beer and pudding match, you could pair it with itself. Bling-wearing gangsta rappers should take a break from champagne and start sipping on this.

Prince of Denmark – Harvey's Brewery. 275ml, 7.5% ABV.
This award-winning stout is a cracking drop to end any evening. It is quite strong and has an acquired taste, but stout lovers would no doubt embrace its complex burnt sugary flavour, with a viscous, yet velvety texture on the palate. To paraphrase Hamlet, 'What a piece of work is stout.'

The Kraken Coffee Stout – Time and Tide Brewing. 440ml, 7.4% ABV. This coffee stout is sensational. The smooth coffee flavour is enriched by the roasted malts and dark chocolate. I found it to be very easy drinking, and certainly didn't taste like a 7.4% ABV beer. This refreshing stout is best served chilled on a hot summer's day. As Liam Neeson's character, Zeus, says in 'Clash of the Titans': "Release the Kraken!"

Full Circle

They say everything in life goes full circle, so perhaps it was no surprise when Guinness released their own Dublin Porter (3.8% ABV) and West Indies Porter (6% ABV), in 2014. They are both brewed in Dublin, but based on 18th-century recipes.

Before starting the next chapter, why not pause for 119 seconds? Cheers.

A SIDEWAYS GLANCE AT WINE IN PUBS

11

WHEN ANYONE is asked how about they became interested in wine, it is normally one wine, on one particular night, which gave them an epiphany. With me, it was an entire region: Burgundy!

We visited Burgundy on holiday in 2006. Most family getaways involve communal activities like camping, walking and arguing. We went wine tasting in France. It was like a National Lampoon's Vacation.

I remember the first vineyard we visited. It was Château de Meursault, in the Côte de Beaune region. A tour of the winery will cost you around 20 euros. The chateau itself was magnificent, but the cellars were even more breathtaking. We were led down some steep stony steps into a 12th-century cellar, full of huge wooden barrels. It was refreshingly cool and quiet. The cellarmaster dipped a long glass rod, which he used to siphon the wine, into one of the oak barrels. As he did so, our tour leader explained:

"That glass rod is often referred to as a wine thief."

I loved that fact. To me, it was like calling a fishing rod a trout burglar. The cellarmaster squirted a sample into everyone's glass. When I received my share, I knew I was meant to peer at it and pontificate, but I felt a tingle of excitement and knocked it back like a shot. The guy said: "Ah, Engleeesh!"

My Stand-Up Show on Wine

Shortly after this trip I began developing a one-man comedy show about wine. In 2007 I performed a one-hour solo show at the Edinburgh Fringe titled, simply, 'Wine.' One of my earliest gags was:

> "I used to write the wine list on a blackboard at my parents' pub. The only problem was I didn't know anything about wine and I couldn't read my Dad's handwriting. So we had such classics as Châteaueuf-du-Pop, Merlin and – my favourite – Peanut Gringo."

I did a preview of this show, where the night was sponsored by a wine shop, but despite giving away FREE WINE, half the audience absconded. I said:

> "How come you guys aren't drinking? Are you all driving?"
> "No. We're recovering alcoholics from the rehab centre round the corner. We came here for a bit of a laugh and didn't know what the show was about."

And I'd just spent an hour telling them about the delights of good wine! One said: "Yes we know how good wine is, that's how we got into this situation in the first place."

One guy did have a glass. He said: "Don't worry about me. I'm a recovering smack addict. I deserve a drink."

Drinking Wine in Pubs

Wine drinkers in pubs fall into two distinct groups: those who like wine to drink on its own, and those who like wine to drink with food.

The nature of wine drinking in pubs has undergone a dramatic transformation since the rise of the gastropubs. When I used to work in pubs in the mid- to late-'90s the selection of wine was limited. There might be a few bottles of white tucked away in the fridge, with a choice of perhaps two white wine styles: dry and medium-dry. Back then most people didn't pay too much attention to the grape when drinking in a pub, but dry usually meant Sauvignon Blanc and medium dry would be a Chardonnay.

Similarly with the reds, I can only recall two wine styles: medium and full-bodied. Medium covered grapes as diverse as Pinot Noir, Merlot or Cabernet Sauvignon. Full-bodied encompassed Syrah, Shiraz, Pinotage, and Malbec.

Finally, there were always a few bottles of classic champagne, like Moët or Bollinger, lurking in the fridge for a celebratory moment, or perhaps a Mateus Rosé for a moderate moment.

Pubs traditionally stocked old-world wine, which is wine predominantly from Europe. The wine labels revealed the place, country of origin, the producer and the year. There was no mention of grape variety. It was presumed you knew a white burgundy was produced from Chardonnay grapes, a red burgundy from Pinot Noir, and a Beaujolais from Gamay, to name but a few. However, the rise of the new-world wines changed everything, particularly with their varietal wines. A varietal wine is one from a single grape variety, and this is usually named on the label. Wines made from more than one grape are called blends. For example, Châteauneuf du Pape is blend of up to 13 different grapes

Chardonnay

Chardonnay was the grape of the choice in the 1990s. It was drunk by young urban professionals, typified by the hilarious Bridget Jones, who was a big fan. She kept her drinks tally at the start of each chapter of her diary, which I always thought was a delightful touch. Australian chardonnay was imported into the UK by the tanker-load and was sold to us as 'Sunshine in a glass'. Perhaps it was this image of drinking Chardonnay in large goblets which gave it a bad name. Snobs were heard to snort "ABC" – anything but Chardonnay. These same snobs would happily drool over a Chablis, which is also Chardonnay, albeit slightly more flinty and minerally in flavour. This reminds me of the classic Basil Fawlty line:

> *"Most people who come in here couldn't tell a Bordeaux from a claret."*

Pinot Grigio and Sauvignon Blanc have since succeeded Chardonnay as the grape of choice for girls on a night out.

Brits' Wine-Drinking Stats

A recent survey by Côtes du Rhône Wines, which quizzed 1,500 Britons about their boozing habits, found that although 91 per cent of men enjoy wine at home, only 24 per cent drink it in the pub. Most men associate the pub with pints of beer. We do enjoy wine with food in the pub, but it is not a drink of choice. This isn't necessarily about manliness. For me, beer quenches my thirst and wine is a treat. Besides, drinking wine in pubs is dangerous, as I drink too quickly, and getting in a round with bottles of wine is potentially apocalyptic. I was once on a stag do where a rugby player, called Casper, gave me a bottle of rosé and said:

> *"Don't worry, I got you a straw. I'm not a monster."*

Wine Measurements

Single glasses of wine were traditionally sold in two measures: standard, which was 175ml, and large, which was 250ml. The latter constitutes one-third of a bottle. A law passed in this country, in 2003, stated that pubs had to offer a small option of 125ml. This measurement equals one unit of alcohol. However, it is almost always cheaper to buy one large glass than two small ones, which defeats the object. As the saying goes, "Go big or go home." Research has shown that one in 10 bars use 250ml as their standard size.

Wine Tax

I was recently in Nantes, in the Loire valley, and a glass of wine was cheaper than a soft drink, meaning it was rude not to have one. French table wine is often sublime, but in the UK you have to spend around £10 to get a decent bottle (at the time of writing). The enormous duty on wine pushes up the price. Did you know 57% of an average-priced bottle of wine is now accounted for by tax? I not only pay my taxes, I drink them.

House Wine

You will always find a wag who claims their favourite wine is house, but I actually think they are on to something. Pubs and restaurants should take pride in the house wine, and provide a quality wine at a reasonable price. If the house is dull and bland, how can you trust the other wines, which you may not have heard of, on the wine list?

My parents' pub opts for two house white wines, both from the same producer: Santa Helena Central Valley, Chile, 2014. The tasting notes say:

> 'The classic Chilean style of Sauvignon Blanc is lively, lifted with a herbal green pea, leafiness & real freshness through the finish – Bottle £12.95; 175ml glass £3.40.'

This is accompanied by a Chilean Chardonnay, also 2014, which could appeal to Goldilocks, as it is described as:

> 'Ripe but not blowsy, rich but not oaked, full-bodied but not overweight, tropical fruit freshness with floral undertones and a bright clean finish – Bottle £12.95; 175 ml glass £3.40.'

Just right!

Choosing Wine

Some people find wine lists a bit intimidating. For those who do, my Aunt told me about her first boyfriend, who hit on an ingenious method of choosing wine in pubs and restaurants. He would simply pick the fourth wine up on the menu. It never let him down. Whatever the venue, whatever the occasion, he would just count four up from the bottom. He called it the Sesame Street Method. To prevent anyone feeling overwhelmed by choice, the wine list in our perfect pub should be on an easy-to-read blackboard – as long as that blackboard is not written by a 13-year-old me, otherwise you will be guzzling peanut gringo.

My White Wine List

Time to put my money where my wine palate is. Choosing a wine list is like picking your perfect England football team; everyone thinks they can do it better than the manager. Here is my wine selection. Feel free to differ, as taste is totally arbitrary. It is a blend of old- and new-world wines.

> MARQUES DE RISCAL, Rueda, Spain, 2014
> THE NED, Sauvignon Blanc, Marlborough, NZ, 2015
> JEFF CARRELL, Morillon Blanc, Chardonnay, Sud-Ouest
>   France, 2013
> LOUIS JADOT, Chablis, France, 2013
> BARON DE ROTHSCHILD, Viognier, France, 2013
> SELLA & MOSCA, Monteoro Vermentino Di Gallura,
>   Sardinia, 2015

I have picked these six wines as my favourites in the £15–£20 range, making them affordable, while still retaining a good profit margin for the landlord.

The Rueda is a simple, easy-drinking, versatile dry Spanish white and a potential house wine. I first discovered it in 10 years ago in Sainsbury's and it was an absolute bargain at £5.99, back then. I even recommended it to a few comedian friends, on dates. (They were embarking on dates, I wasn't dating comedians and recommending it.)

The Ned is a classic Sauvignon Blanc in the Kiwi style, fruity, aromatic, and best served chilled on a summer's day. I first had this at a wine tasting at Lord's Cricket Ground, and it has the perfect line and length. At the time of writing, Co-op are promoting it at £6.99, reduced from £9.99. This is another good-value wine and one of my Leo's favourites. Incidentally, I picked this in favour of a Sancerre, as I think it would suit the relaxed pub environment a little more.

Likewise, I am a big fan of white burgundies, such as Corton-Charlemagne, Le Montrachet (the Ts are silent) and Bâtard-Montrachet (not its illegitimate, or even offensive brother). If this were a restaurant wine list, they would be one of the first on the team sheet. But, this being a pub list, I thought I would plump for a delicious Chardonnay from south-west France, Burgundian in style, but at least half the price of its famous neighbours. Morillon Blanc is a beautiful golden colour, full-bodied, with a buttery honey flavour. I discovered it by chance, while perusing and tasting wine at Avery's in Bristol. I bought a couple of bottles for my Aunt's birthday. She has since adopted it as her 'house wine' at home, and bought their entire stock. They were once out, so rather than risk it, she now orders in bulk.

Vermentino is a luscious grape from Sardinia, which I first discovered on holiday, many years ago. As I write, Vermentino is becoming the new chic wine style of choice, and is currently the house white at the Soho House group. Sella & Mosca Monteoro Vermentino Di Gallura 2015 is perfect example. It is £9.95 a bottle online, so could still be sold in a pub at a reasonable price.

Champagne and Sparkling Wine

On the fizz front, it would also be good to provide a range of styles and prices. Champagne can only be classified as such if it has been made from grapes grown in the Champagne region, and in a certain style, known as *Méthode Champenoise*, which requires a secondary fermentation in the bottle. Everywhere else, it is simply known as sparkling wine.

Champagne is a blend of Chardonnay, Pinot Noir and Pinot Meunier grapes. Blanc de Blancs, a French term meaning white from whites, is champagne made from 100 per cent Chardonnay.

Most champagne made today is non-vintage, which means it is a blend of grapes from different years. I know vintage champagne sounds classier, but all it means is that the grapes were blended from a single year. If a year is unfavourable, non-vintage champagne allows a level of guaranteed quality and consistency, by mixing grapes from different years.

Finally, a *Cuvée De Prestige* is considered to be top of the range by a champagne house. Famous examples include Louis Roederer's Cristal, Laurent-Perrier's Grand Siècle, Moët & Chandon's Dom Pérignon, and Pol Roger's Cuvée Sir Winston Churchill. Most of which you may heard name-checked in a gangsta rap track.

A glass of champagne is a beautiful sight, but originally it was a cloudy drink, because of all the yeast. Veuve Cliquot was an actual person. The French word *Veuve* means widow. Madame Cliquot was a remarkable woman; she lived from 1777 to 1866, and was known as the Grande Dame of Champagne. She was credited with inventing the process of riddling. This involves storing the bottles on a slant and giving each individual bottle a slight turn every so often. By doing so, the left-over yeast and sediment, from the wine's secondary fermentation, eventually settles in the bottle's neck. This yeast and sediment explodes when a bottle is opened. So during the process of *dégorgement*, as the French call it, you are purifying the champagne, and not losing any of the good stuff.

Champagne is best served in flutes. However, the coupe, a saucer-shaped bowl with a small stem, is still popular in

France and the United States. Legend has it that the shape was based on the left breast of Marie Antoinette, making it a saucy-shaped bowl. Thirsty Americans could do worse than design a champagne bowl based on Kim Kardashian's left buttock. Perhaps call it a 'Booty Bowl'. Over to you Kanye.

When it comes to sparkling wine, Prosecco is the flavour of the moment. It is refreshing, fun and reasonably priced. This Italian wine has two variants: *spumante*, a rather unsavoury word for sparkling, and *frizzante*, which means semi-sparkling. Tanners produces a fine Prosecco and this would kick off my sparklers.

> TANNERS, Prosecco Brut, Treviso, Italy NV
> Sparkling Vouvray
> POL ROGER Champagne

On the previously mentioned trip to Nantes, Leo and I drank our own bodyweight in sparkling Vouvray. You may purchase a decent bottle in the local supermarket for only five euros, and it tastes delicious. Johnny Depp famously filled a bathtub with champagne for Kate Moss. Vouvray makes it possible for any Johnny to do so.

My list would not be complete without Pol Roger as my top-line champagne. It is a classy, yet unpretentious, champagne, and the choice for Kate and Wills' wedding. I also spotted Walter White crack open a bottle of Winston Churchill Cuvée in the hit television series 'Breaking Bad.'

My Red Wine List

Like many folk, I enjoy a white wine but, after a glass or two, I like to hit the reds. These are my pub red wines of choice:

> ROARING MEG Pinot Noir, Mt Difficulty, Central Otago, 2013
> JOSEPH DROUHIN Côte de Nuits Villages, 2014
> LA MONEDA RESERVA MALBEC, Central Valley, Chile, 2015
> CHÂTEAU MUSAR

Some people rate New Zealand for the Sauvignons, but I prefer to rave about their reds, in particular their pinots, from Central Otago in the South Island. Roaring Meg is bursting with cherry and blackberry flavours with a hint of vanilla. This is a beautiful wine and dangerously moreish.

A few years ago I went on another wine trip to Beaune, which is perhaps the home of old-world Pinot Noir. I drank – sorry, tasted – with my Dad and his cohorts. The group comprised 17 septuagenarians and me, and they are part of a Bristolian fine-dining fraternity called The Pink Elephant Club. The pinkest thing about them is their noses. We visited some incredible wineries, from Château Meursault to Château Pommard. This was my second visit to Meursault and, this time, I resisted necking my wine like a shot.

On the last day we had a tour of Joseph Drouhin's cellars. Our guide showed us a false wall behind which the Drouhin family hid their most-valued wines when the Nazis occupied Beaune during the World War II. I loved this story and pictured the scenario:

"Maman, the Germans are coming!"
"Quick children, hide the booze."

Côtes de Nuits Villages is an easy-drinking Burgundy. You can really taste cherries and truffles. I felt the wine is far more practical for a pub than the more pricey Gevrey-Chambertin and Chambolle-Musigny.

Malbec has risen in popularity in the last few years. It has long been a favourite in the French region of Cahors, but the Argentines have adopted it as their national varietal of choice. As keen purveyors of steak, you can see why they identify with it so much. I was lucky enough to visit Argentina and, like France, their local wines are far classier, more exciting and cheaper than their imported counterparts.

I chose the 2015 La Moneda Reserva Malbec from Central

Valley in Chile as it was awarded Best in Show in the single-varietal red under-£15 category at the 2016 Decanter World Wine Awards. Not only that, it retails at £4.37 in Asda! 'Pocket the difference' as their slogan used to say. Often the only true method of assessing a wine is to taste it blind; most of us are susceptible to giving the benefit of the doubt to a wine we already know is expensive or famous, and dismissing a cheap one. Judges praised the wine for flavours of:

> *'Freshly crushed black fruit, creamy vanilla yoghurt and pepper spice.'*

This is a real bargain and would have to be a strong candidate for house red.

I deliberated over my final choice. I could have flown in the face of wine snob Miles, from the film 'Sideways', and picked a Chilean Merlot, but while I enjoy a drop, most are available at the supermarket and the point of going to the pub is to drink something you would not drink at home.

So I plumped for Château Musar, a delightful wine from the Lebanon. You might not think of the Lebanon as a rich source of wine, despite Jesus' miraculous wine-making skills. This famous winery is based 15 miles north of Beirut and bravely continued production despite civil war. Legend has it that its founder, Gaston Hochar, avoided calls to hide in an air raid shelter during a bombing campaign near his house, but instead cracked open a bottle of his favourite Musar and settled down to a good book. What a classy guy! Who says the Brits are the only ones with a stiff upper lip and the Dunkirk spirit?

Hochar founded Château Musar in 1930, after returning from Bordeaux, but it didn't achieve notoriety until 1979, when it was coveted in the Bristol Wine Fair. It is a beautiful wine, blending Cabernet Sauvignon and Carignan, bringing a Middle Eastern exoticism to a Bordeaux style, giving it the nickname 'The Lafitte of the Lebanon." I love it and think it's a perfect wine to give my list a more eclectic feel.

The most exciting aspect about wine is that, like real ale, it is a living, breathing, thing. It's alive. Every wine is individual and tells a story, which gives it a delightful sense of mystery. There is nothing like opening an old bottle of wine and waiting to find out whether it tastes as good as you hope. Last Christmas, I overheard a close family friend, Sian, instruct her husband:

> *"Oh Bob, don't bother with those old dusty bottles of wine, we've got guests, treat them to some new ones!"*

SHEEP DIP AND PIG'S NOSE WHISKY

12

WHISKY IN GAELIC is 'uisge beatha', which means 'water of life.' So when some folk ask for water in their whisky, maybe they are really angling for a free top up.

A good whisky selection is a must in any serious pub. The farmers in my local village pub, where I grew up in the West Country, would always end the evening with a few leisurely drams to send them on their way.

Scotch whisky is big business. According to www.scotch-whisky.org.uk:

> 'Overall, Scotch whisky represents around 85% of Scottish food and drink exports and nearly a quarter of the British total. The industry's exports are worth £135 a second to the UK trade balance.'

That is an incredible stat and just proves how huge the Scotch whisky industry really is. Little wonder the UK was so reluctant to let Scotland achieve their independence.

The Angels' Share

There is a mischievous Scottish film about whisky, worth watching, called *Angels' Share*. It was directed by Ken Loach in 2012. Without giving away any of the plot, the title refers to a process in which whisky stored in barrels gradually evaporates at an approximate rate of 2% a year, and this is affectionately called 'The Angels' Share'. This celestial liquid is usually about 40% proof, which means the Holy Spirit has quite a kick. No wonder it's so naughty in the Bible. If Red Bull gives you wings, this will make your body soar and your head sore.

I appreciate the whole nature of whisky: the aroma, the smoky flavours, its strength, its history and all the different variations. However, I have a confession to make: I am not so keen on the taste. I know – W.T.F. – Whisky Tango Foxtrot! (Incidentally, that's three ingredients of a classic F. Scott Fitzgerald night out.) It is a shame, because I like the idea of drinking whisky, especially nursing a glass by a crackling open log fire on a cold winter's night. Without wishing to compare it to Marmite, whisky is an acquired taste and the folk who do like it, love it.

Whisky Comedy Shows

In 2014 I teamed up with Vladimir McTavish, a wonderful Scottish comedian and whisky aficionado. We toured a show about wine and whisky called 'The Grape and the Grain'. I championed wine, while Vlad waxed lyrical on whisky. Vlad's passion and enthusiasm was infectious. I loved listening to his stories every night and learnt a lot on the subject.

A few years ago I was interviewed about whisky for a video cast by a hirsute Glaswegian comedian, Alan Anderson. It was slightly strange to be talking about a subject I had no intention of trying. It was probably the nearest I will ever feel to being a wily politician. Alan was performing a show at the Fringe called 'Whisky Fir Dummies'. It was only £7 for a ticket and you could try as much as you would like, which was a pretty sweet deal. I brought along a good friend, Jon Richardson. Jon is a cracking comedian, a man of taste and a discerning drinker. I savoured the aroma of my share, then passed my glass to Jon. I sniffed, he sniftered. He was being treated to free whisky all night and beaming. He wasn't the only one. There were more red noses in that room than at a Santa convention on Comic Relief Day.

Family Whisky

Whisky is perhaps the most important drink in my family. In the mid-1970s my Dad had the opportunity to produce his own Scotch whisky. A friend of his offered him the rights to a recipe and my Dad thought a whisky, particular to his pub, would be a delightful touch on the top shelf. So in 1974 a new malt whisky hit the optics. He needed a catchy name, so adopted the nickname the local farmers gave to whisky, Sheep Dip. To his surprise, it sold very well. One day, a Bristolian distributor by the name of Francis Pearson asked if he could sell it and entered it into a competition. It won and was soon flying off the shelves at Harrods, where it was a top-selling malt whisky for nine years.

The Story of Sheep Dip

This is my Dad's story, so I thought I would interview him, and let him tell you directly.

DAD: *"I think I was the first person to give an unusual name to a brand of spirit. Previously, all whisky names were from hallowed geographical locations such as Speyside or Glenfiddich. They were all treated with such reverence. I actually chose the name Sheep Dip because I wanted to have some fun."*

JAMES: *"How did it all come about?"*

DAD: *"Well, when I was running the pub, we had a range of malt whiskies behind the bar. They all began with Glen. Glenfarquis, Glenfiddich, Glenmorangie. In those days, people didn't know one from the other, so I thought we'd have a little fun, and we'd have our own malt whisky and I'd give it an unusual name.*

*The idea came to me as many of the boys in the public bar were
mostly farmers and quite a lot of them were sheep farmers,
and at the end of the evening they would always finish off
with a couple of glasses of whisky each. They would
invariably say "I'll have another drop of that there Sheep Dip."
And that's what they called it. So I thought I'd call it Sheep Dip.
I registered the name and Sheep Dip it was."*

JAMES: *"Who actually distilled the whisky?"*

DAD: *"I was at the Grand Hotel in Bristol, and was introduced
to a man called Tim Morrison. He was the son of Stanley
Morrison, a Glaswegian whisky broker, who had two malt
whiskies, Bowmore and Glen Garioch."*

JAMES: *"Another Glen."*

DAD: *"Yes indeed. I told Tim that I wanted to produce my own
Sheep Dip whisky. He said it was sacrilege to call it that.
I said, I wanted a name to have a little bit of fun with.
He said, You want to bottle it as well? I said, Yes. After a while,
he said, I'll tell you what I'll do, providing you have it bottled
in Scotland, I'll choose a blended malt whisky for you to
put in Sheep Dip. It will be bottled in Scotland and we'll put
the Sheep Dip label on."*

JAMES: *"So, it was like an own-brand whisky."*

DAD: *"Yes. It was S. P. Morrison's malt whisky in our bottles."*

There we have it, straight from the Sheep Dip's mouth.

The Aftermath of Sheep Dip

At the height of its fame a weekly cartoon ran in *The Sunday
Times* about the villagers of Oldbury on Severn and their
adventures with whisky.

Sheep Dip became a cult hit and even has its own fan club, who meet up wearing official Sheep Dip knitted sweaters.

My favourite Sheep Dip story emerged from Somerset, where farmers allegedly marked down 'Sheep Dip' on their tax returns as a legitimate farming expense.

The whisky sales had its perks. In 1990 we were lucky enough to go on a family holiday to California. San Francisco blew my tiny mind: cable cars tobogganing down the very streets of a Dirty Harry car chase; the Golden Gate Bridge, gleaming and majestic; the City Lights bookshop, where the Jack Kerouac legend began; Oakland A's baseball; beat boxing; and huge family meals.

Our most memorable meal was at a place called The Fog City Diner. We caught a cab from Union Square up to the dock area. It was situated on Battery Street, not far from Pier 23. The restaurant sign was lit up in neon. It was a popular tourist hotspot and occasional film location. I recognised it from *So I Married an Axe Murderer*, with Mike Myers. The diner was dripping with 1930s chic, chequered tiles and stainless steel fittings. I am a messy eater at the best of times, so ribs, while delicious, was a dangerous choice and my face was soon covered in barbecue sauce.

While at the bar, my Dad spotted a bottle of Sheep Dip on the optics and mentioned his connection to the barman. Within seconds, the waiter was joyously addressing us as Mr and Mrs Sheep Dip and the little Sheep Dips. He told us that two weeks previously Keifer Sutherland and Julia Roberts had been in. Keifer had hit the Sheep Dip pretty hard and had to be carried out. His sheep had been dunked, rather than dipped. My first brush with fame was my Dad inadvertently poisoning a famous Hollywood actor.

Pig's Nose

In 1981 my Dad followed up the success of Sheep Dip with his tricky second album, a blended whisky, called Pig's Nose. It took him three years to conjure up the name. The by-line on the label read:

'Tis said the whisky is as soft and smooth as a Pig's Nose.'

Granted, it was an unusual name, but it also sold well. I remember driving through the Cotswolds and my Dad pulled up at a lay-by, pointed at the next bend and proclaimed: "I was driving round the next corner when I thought up the name Pig's Nose."

So, not only was it an unusual name, but when my Dad conceived it, he was quite literally around the bend. Our family dubbed that bend 'Pig's Nose Corner'.

Scotch Whisky

There are some delicious names given to Scotch whisky, all of which would have to be in our perfect pub. Allow the following poetical names to roll around your mouth like a Cuban cigar: Laphroaig, Glenmorangie, Glenfiddich and – my favourite – Talisker. For most of these you have to make a 'whisky face' to pronounce them.

The name Teachers has always tickled me. It's the opposite of Jack Daniels. Is there a least-sexy profession to attach itself to a brand of liquor?

> *"A shot of Accountant please landlord. Just one.*
> *Actually, make it a double entry, with a receipt."*

Although, you could probably have fun with a bottle of Quantity Surveyor.

Whisky vs Whiskey

It is only an 'e', but it is extremely important. Whisky refers to Scotch, whereas whiskey denotes Irish and American liquors. Get this wrong in Glasgow, at your peril. (Please note, the plural of whisky is whiskies and the plural of whiskey is whiskeys.)

To complicate matters, Canadian and Japanese producers also spell whisky without an 'e'. American drinks journalist, Nora Maynard, introduced a fun mnemonic, in an article for thekitch.com. She suggested countries with an 'e' in them spell it whiskey, and countries without an 'e' – Scotland, Canada and Japan – spell it whisky. Her suggestion is probably as good a general rule as we can hope to get, although the issue is obviously not clear cut.

Good job we order verbally at the bar!

Jack Daniel's

I suppose our pub would have to stock Jack Daniel's, just for the trendies, who are sucked in by the rock 'n' roll marketing image. JD and coke may be a popular party drink, but trying ordering that in the highlands of Scotland.

Although Jack Daniel's is the top selling American whiskey in the world, its home county is actually a dry state. Maybe it's this fact that gives this Tennessee bourbon its rebellious image. The adverts focus on its quirky founder, old Jack Daniel, his independence and how he protected his distillery. Associating JD with a maverick nature and an independent spirit was a master stroke which makes it relevant, romantic, rock 'n' roll, and irresistible to the youth worldwide. Their brand image focuses on defiance and the herd lap it up, quite literally. No Sheep Dip knitted sweaters for rock 'n' roll bands like Guns N' Roses, or Motley Crue. ZZ Top might be able to pull it off though.

Whiskey Cocktails

Whiskey cocktails have had a resurgence of late. A friend of ours, Jamie Berger, who launched Pitt Cue, a former pop-up turned restaurant focusing on American-style pit barbecue, specialises in whiskey cocktails. They are dangerously delicious.

Although I eschew straight Scotch, I am quite partial to a whiskey cocktail and think they are a fun addition to any bar. Here's a few to wet your whiskey whistle.

Whiskey Sour

Many whiskey cocktails were conceived in America in the late-19th century. The whiskey sour is the granddaddy of whiskey cocktails and head of the sour family. It became popular in the mid-19th century and many other cocktails were influenced by it, or used it as a base to start from.

INGREDIENTS:
4.5 cl (3 parts) Bourbon whiskey
3 cl (2 parts) fresh lemon juice
1.5 cl (1 part) gomme syrup
dash egg white (optional)

Old Fashioned

The Old Fashioned was said to be invented in Kentucky in 1881. A bartender prepared it in honour of Colonel James E. Pepper at the Pendennis Club. Pepper, a whiskey distiller, took the recipe and made it famous at the Waldorf Astoria in New York City. It is served in a tumbler known as an Old Fashioned glass, after the drink.

INGREDIENTS:

1 sugar cube

3 dashes Angostura bitters

1 dash club soda

2 oz. rye whiskey

1 old-fashioned glass

Manhattan

The Manhattan is made from whiskey, sweet vermouth and bitters. For a real Manhattan you need rye whiskey. (A Rob Roy is the same recipe using scotch.) It is one of five cocktails named after New York City's five boroughs.

INGREDIENTS:

2 oz. rye whiskey

1 oz. Italian vermouth

2 dashes Angostura bitters

1 cocktail glass

Hot Toddies

Finally I think a delightful winter addition would be the Hot Toddy, also known as the Hot Totty. There are several different recipes; my favourite is whisky, hot water, a slice of raw ginger, honey and lemon. It's a healthy spirit, to ward off the evil ones. We serve Bloody Marys to nurse a hangover, so why not tackle a cold or chill with a similar remedy. The blackboard slogan could be:

'Is your Man Flu man enough to tackle some Hot Totty?'

The Anchor's Whisky Selection

I quizzed my Dad on his approach to stocking whisky at The Anchor. He said:

> "The Anchor has 80 different whiskies, but we have a tremendous local following and the regulars love having a change of whisky. We have a whisky bible by the bar and they can read up about it. It's a full tome with the stories behind all 80 whiskies on offer. We have one for gin too."

"80 whiskies?" I replied, "You could go right around the bar, four and a half times a year, if you had one a day."

Our Perfect Whisky Selection

Our perfect pub should contain a wide range of whiskies and whiskeys for the aficionados. We also require an abundance of bourbon, for the young fashionable folk with their whiskey cocktails. As an antidote for overindulgence, why not serve Blood Marys with bourbon to recharge the batteries, and Hot Toddies to raise you from your sickbed and back to the bar.

CHIN CHIN FOR GIN

13

GIN HAS RECENTLY had a resurgence, but it has always been a party spirit.

My friend Stinger once had a White Spirits party. Unfortunately, this wasn't a glorification of all things gin and vodka, he had just had a new carpet installed and was terrified of red wine spillages.

Gin Lyrics in Music and Poetry

When T. S. Eliot was asked where he drew his inspiration from, he replied,

"Gin and drugs dear lady, gin and drugs."

Sounds like a soundbite from a Gallagher brother, whilst feeling 'Supersonic'.

There have been some classic songs extolling the virtues of gin including Divine Comedy's 'Gin Soaked Boy', and Snoop Doggy Dogg's 'Gin and juice'. The Ramones screamed about their favourite gin in 'Somebody Put Something in My Drink,' which contains the couplet:

'Tanqueray and tonic's my favourite drink
I don't like anything coloured pink.'

So the Ramones were not only anti-establishment, but also anti-pink gin: the two rebellious pillars of society.

History of Gin

Before delving into gin, we must first appreciate its history.

Gin is a flavoured white spirit, the key ingredient of which is the juniper berry. So much so, even the word gin was derived from the Latin word *juniperus*, which sounds like a condition in which you crave gin.

"James was very 'juniperus' this evening."

Gin was 'ori-GIN-ally' invented by the Dutch and popularised by the English. So in linguistic terms, the Latin word juniperus became the Dutch word jenever and the olde English word genever, from which we derive the word gin. I appreciate this is a bit of a mouthful; my advice is – don't drink and derive.

I quite like the word juniper, it has a lovely ring to it. I'm sure an old school comedian would have fun with it:

"Juniper?"
"Nip her? I didn't even bite her." Boom-tish!

Incredibly, gin was originally used in Holland as a herbal medicine, treating conditions such as gout and liver failure. So, medically speaking, gin could be considered the ultimate hair of the dog. How we love those free-thinking Dutch folk. But this is not as crazy as it sounds. A Dutch scientist discovered that juniper oil was a good herbal remedy. Some other bright spark paired it to a distilled spirit, and added botanicals to make it more palatable. At this stage, it was only available from apothecaries, so claims of reported illnesses soared, as folk tried to acquire bottles of this rare genever spirit. Entrepreneurs soon realised its sales potential and small distilleries were set up to cope with demand.

Gin became internationally renowned during the Thirty Years War (1618–1648), during which the English fought alongside the Dutch. The English troops were impressed by the bravery of the Dutch, which was attributed to their performance-enhancing drug, gin. Gin bottles were even part of their battle regalia; they hung from their utility belts like a drunken Batman on a night out. Gin calmed and soothed the nerves of terrified troops. Returning soldiers regaled stories of 'Dutch Courage' and spread the word about the great god of gin. This was free advertising for the Dutch, which enabled them to export their invention worldwide.

As briefly referred to in Chapter 2 on the history of pubs, when William of Orange ascended to the throne he decided to make gin the drink of the realm. In 1690, he decreed that anyone could distil gin, as long as it was produced from homegrown English corn. Secondly, he increased tax on beer. The net result was that while beer became more expensive, gin prices plummeted. William had his wish, gin was in.

Mother's Ruin

By the early 18th century, gin was ubiquitous, and there were around 7,000 gin shops in London. Cheap gin, or 'Bathtub Gin' as it was known, was made from low-quality grain, but still packed a punch. Thomas Carlyle disparagingly referred to it as 'Liquid madness.' According to *The Spirit of Gin* by Matt Teacher, the rise in gin consumption was startling. He quotes the following figures:

1684: 524,000 gallons
1700: 1,223,000 gallons
1710: 2,000,000 gallons
1730: 3,000,000 gallons
1735: 6,000,000 gallons
1743: 8,000,000 gallons

To put this into perspective, howmanywiki.com estimates there are 153 UK shots to a gallon. So in 1743, our English ancestors downed 1,224,000,000 or 1.2 billion shots. Now that is binge drinking.

Rather than becoming the discerning English tipple of the gentry that William of Orange had anticipated, it became the crutch of the poor. In city slums it was safer to drink gin rather than risking water which was polluted and carried disease.

William Hogarth's famous painting 'Gin Lane' depicted a debauched view of London, supposedly caused by 'Mother's Ruin'. I imagine gin was a welcome release from the intolerable hardships suffered by the poor, rather than a cause. If you had to sleep with your head on a slack of rope, in a crowded workhouse, after a hard day's graft, you might need a slug of gin to lull you to sleep.

By the mid-18th century gin consumption had reached epidemic proportions and the government finally intervened. Gin Acts were passed, in which a licence was required in order to sell alcohol. This signalled the death knell for most unlicensed dram shops. However, it is tricky to shut down an entire industry, and cheap gin went underground. It re-emerged in a sweeter recipe, known as 'Old Tom Gin'. If you wanted to score some Old Tom, you had to seek out a shop sporting the symbol of a black cat; this presumably was Old Tom himself. Trust a cat to ignore authority and remain defiantly independent.

Although Old Tom allegedly tasted sweeter, it was still far from a delicacy. It was occasionally flavoured with turpentine. Flavoured is perhaps the wrong word; cut with turps is more appropriate, like some hooky cocaine. I'm told turps gives gin a woody taste. I would love to hear a pretentious drinks expert critiquing it:

> "Hmmm. I'm getting rotten plywood. Tastes like the bottom of a garden shed in bleak midwinter. Ooh. I can almost feel a splinter on my tongue. Unmistakably Old Tom."

Fast forward to the early-19th century and gin had become the choice tipple of the gentry. It was an incredible turna-

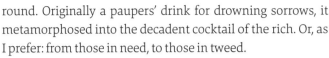

round. Originally a paupers' drink for drowning sorrows, it metamorphosed into the decadent cocktail of the rich. Or, as I prefer: from those in need, to those in tweed.

Aside from the fall-out of the gin acts, there were three reasons for this change. The first was the invention of the distillation column, which led to a purer, smoother, better-quality gin. This meant gin was able to be paired with subtler botanicals other than just juniper, which opened up a whole new world of flavour combinations. Now producers were experimenting with all manner of botanicals including coriander, cinnamon and mint, to name but a few.

London Dry

This new smoother gin became known as London Dry. It is important to note that London Dry refers to the style, rather than the place of origin. London Dry can be produced anywhere. Plymouth gin however, can only be regarded as such if it was made in Plymouth. It's a bit like the rule that only sparkling wine made in the Champagne region can be called champagne.

Quinine and the Medicinal Qualities of Gin and Tonic

The second reason for the upper classes embracing gin was its medicinal qualities. The quinine in tonic is supposedly good for preventing malaria. They used it as a treatment in colonial India, but it has a sharp taste, so colonials used to slip a shot of gin in to make it more palatable. Legend has it that British officers in India decided that instead of downing their medicine at dawn, with the troops, they would imbibe theirs in a more gentlemanly manner, by taking them as cocktails at sundown. Back then, a tickly cough could lead to an all-night session:

"Sore throat? I know just the thing, my good fellow.
Wrap your neck in your finest cravat and join me for
a sundowner of gin and cod liver oil. Pip old bean."

Mosquitoes seem to have re-emerged in this country, due to global warming, so maybe we should all be drinking stronger quantities of quinine in our gin and tonics.

Quinine is sourced naturally from the bark of the cinchona tree, in the Peruvian Andes. This description makes it sound like an ingredient to be added to a cauldron.

Incidentally, the colloquial name for the cinchona tree is fever tree, which inspired the brand name for 'Fever-Tree' tonic water.

Alongside quinine, the navy discovered a new cure for sea sickness, angostura bitters. Like the British officers in colonial India, they decided their medicine tasted far more civilised with gin. Thus, in 1824, 'Pink Gin' came into being. It was the year that the Royal Navy turned pink. I'm sure the Ramones would have been disgusted.

My Dad served in the Merchant Navy for three years and was even ship's doctor for a few voyages. He had no real medical training, but his years running pubs proved to be useful. All that was required, in his role as ship's doctor, was a medical dictionary and a plentiful supply of gin, tonic and angostura bitters. His medicine cabinet was in fact a drinks cabinet. He told me a delightful story of dropping anchor at a dry port in India. With a ban on alcohol, he registered himself and three shipmates as alcoholics. They were promptly supplied with a welcome remedy – 12 bottles of India Pale Ale.

Bombay Sapphire

Intriguingly, Bombay Sapphire gin is not from India at all, but originated in England in 1987. I know. I was shocked too. Those menacing, marketing folk have hoodwinked us again.

However, it was inspired by gin's popularity in colonial India; the label even has a picture of Queen Victoria to give it historical overtones. The bottle is sapphire coloured. In fact, most old gins were sold in colourful bottles, as gin was cloudy before the invention of column stills.

The last consequence of the upper classes embracing gin was the arrival of ornate and exquisite gin palaces which, as I mentioned in Chapter 2, were the forerunners to the Victorian pub style.

Gin Cocktails

Gin has always been in demand as the base liquor for a plethora of cocktails, including the classic Gin Martini, Gimlet, Negroni, and the Singapore Sling. The latter was made famous at Raffles Hotel and has 11 ingredients. However, I can't imagine many pub folk ordering a Singapore Sling on a wet Wednesday night:

> *"Sorry I took so long at the bar, I got stuck behind the bloke in bright red trousers and sunglasses on his head, ordering a pair of Singapore Slings. It's fine to reminisce about your Far East jaunt, but why couldn't they do it with a couple bottles of Tiger?"*

In the mid-1980s my Dad decided he wanted to stock his own gin behind the bar and contacted a colleague to commission it. Was my father's gin medicinal? If so, I worry, as it was called Greencock Gin. Still, what happens in the merchant navy, stays in the merchant navy.

Last year, I was hosting a comedy show in Cardiff, and asked a stag where his wife-to-be was celebrating. He revealed she was at a gin tasting in London Bridge. "Little Bird on Maltby Street?" I inquired.

"Yes!" he said, "How do you know?"

He was gobsmacked. Truth be told, Little Bird is run by one of Leo's friends.

New Wave of Gin

Gin is currently very much in fashion. In fact, the new wave of gin distillers mirrors the rise in craft ales. The reason for this is that the price of a copper still has come down in recent years, which has made the dream of producing your own gin slightly more affordable and doable. Small gin distillers have benefitted in a similar manner to microbrewers: the batch can made be a lot smaller, and the freedom of information that the internet has provided has fast-tracked the gin enthusiast from home brewer to professional distiller. Finally, the foodie movement has provided us with better quality botanicals than ever before. For example, Monkey 47 gin achieved its name because it has 47 botanicals in it. Eat your monkey heart out, Singapore Sling.

Gin is made using a still with connecting pipes, which makes the apparatus look like a cross between a huge tuba and a mad scientist's chemistry set. Subterranean hipsters often use the copper stills and make them the centrepiece of the bar. Why not? They're beautiful. In 'hipsterville' they are the coffee-making equivalent of the 1960s Gaggia coffee machine you often see in trendy independent coffee shops.

Our primary concern is what makes the perfect pub, so a distillery, even a small one, might be impractical. The Four Thieves pub in Battersea has a microdistillery. They have 45 gins on offer, besides their own, and a drinking area referred to as the Gin Yard. I like the phrase 'Gin Yard'; it sounds like a drunken measurement.

> "It took me three hours to get home. It was only 800 yards, but those yards were gin yards."

Gin Masterclass

A cocktail bar recently opened near our house and I spotted a blackboard advertising a gin masterclass. For a mere £10, it would be rude not to. It was hosted by a charismatic mixologist called Marc Stagg. He certainly looked the part, in a designer waistcoat and black tie with a pin. Marc talked us through the history and trends of gin, before unleashing our creativity and tasking us to create our very own cocktails.

Marc asked loads of questions. We were all quiet to start with, but warmed up as the gin flowed. In all these type of events, there is always someone who wants to get a little too involved. In our case, there was a lady whose personality was as loud as her clothes. The problem is it prevents everyone else from joining in.

The event promoted Blue Bottle gin, a delightfully smooth dry gin, from Jersey. The cocktail Leo and I created required 50ml of Blue Bottle gin. We used a mixing jug, which looked like an ornate glass vase. We filled this with ice. The most important part of any gin cocktail is keeping it cold. We added 20ml of pink grapefruit juice and a glob of honey for balance. The botanical we chose was fresh mint.

Marc had demonstrated 'The Slap', which was his stylised method of prepping the herb. You place some mint in the palm of your hand and slap with the other. It makes a great sound and you look like a real showman behind the bar. Slapping the mint releases all the flavour.

Lastly, Leo added a pinch of salt. She loves to season. To finish, we poured it through the strainer in to a glass, thus separating our cocktail from the botanicals and ice. We tasted our creation by dipping in a plastic straw. The gin taste was a little predominant, so we added another 30ml of pink grapefruit juice.

Finally, the moment of truth. Before critiquing, Marc asked the name of our cocktail. 'The Leonora' I answered. After all, she had done most of the work. I was merely an assistant, a mixologist's mate. Marc decreed it tasted refreshing, but it was a little watery, as the ice had been in too long. In our defence, we were waiting for the tea strainer to do a double strain. I suppose a bad cocktail maker blames waiting for his tools. Marc also suggested that if we had given it a whirl in the cocktail shaker the flavours would have blossomed more.

It turns out The Leonora wasn't as unique as we had hoped. Unwittingly, Marc revealed, we had created, or recreated, a Hemingway Daiquiri. So, I'd say we were clearly on the right lines! All in all, it was a top night out and the only way to finish an evening like that is to head home and put on the Tom Cruise classic, 'Cocktail'.

Being presented with The Leonora...   our glowing faces afterwards.

Gin Selection in Our Perfect Pub

So now we know a little about gin, the question is, which brands should we stock in our perfect pub? The first point of order is to pick a house gin. Whenever you order a gin and tonic at a bar you will be served the house gin, unless you specify.

I think the house gin needs to be classy, yet mainstream. Personally, I would follow the Ramones and pick Tanqueray, but you may prefer Gordon's, Hendrick's, Bombay Sapphire or Beefeater.

My Dad's thoughts on stocking gin in his pub are:

"People like choice. Gin is the drink of the moment. A dozen gins are quite enough to choose from. Have various different botanical flavours and price. The Anchor's house gin is No. 6 because it is distilled locally."

When it comes to gin, it is all about offering an exciting range.

Three Gins to Try

1 **Monkey** 47 (47% ABV) – worth sampling to see if you can decipher the 47 botanicals, mentioned earlier. One of the 47 is a rather unique ingredient, cranberries. This is more than a gimmick, as it is widely regarded as one of the best gins around. It is made in Germany's Black Forest, by Schwarzwald. I imagine we can guess their favourite number.

2 **Tarquin's** Cornish Dry Gin (42% ABV) – an award-winning modern take on the classic London Dry style. This gin is the passion of one man, Tarquin Leadbetter, a classically trained chef from the Cordon Bleu institute in Paris, who set up Cornwall's first distillery in over 100 years. It is distilled with 12 botanicals, including hand-picked violets, controversially sourced from Devon, but grown in Tarquin's own back garden.

3 **Sipsmith's** London Dry Gin (41.6% ABV) – established in London in 2009. In fact, it is the first copper pot distillery to start up in London for 189 years. They named their copper pot Prudence. Its 10 botanicals are blended with Lydwell Spring Water, from the spring that is the source of the River Thames.

Fever-Tree Tonic Water

When it comes to gin and tonic, the aforementioned Fever-Tree would be my tonic water of choice in our perfect pub. It was only launched in the UK in 2005, but since then has taken the market by storm. It is certainly a favourite in my house. Fever-Tree contains no artificial sweeteners or preservatives, which in today's health-conscious society is crucial to our well-being. According to their website, the tasting notes for Fever-Tree Indian tonic water go as follows:

'The highest quality quinine was sourced from the Rwanda Congo Border and blended with sorting water and eight

botanical flavours, including rare ingredients such as
marigold extracts and a bitter orange from Mexico.'

These are similar descriptors for gin and they make the two obvious bedfellows. It seems their attention to detail and use of naturally sourced ingredients gives Fever-Tree the winning edge.

World Gin Day

Since 2009 the second Saturday in June has been designated World Gin Day. We have to commemorate this date in our perfect pub. One of the most memorable gin and tonics I have imbibed was with my Dad and his pals, in San Sebastian, in Spain's Basque country, and it arrived in a huge goblet laden with ice, like a gin Slush Puppie. We should definitely celebrate this day Spanish style.

As the Japanese say, "Chin" or, to be more in keeping with this chapter, "Gin Gin".

THE DREADED TOP SHELF, BEHIND THE BAR

14

A FTER A FEW BEERS, some drinkers' eyes stray towards the top shelf. This maverick move makes me wince. In my imperfect pub, the spirits section resembles an apothecary's medicine cabinet. Dusty potion bottles, which look like they should prescribed rather than imbibed, stare down at you menacingly. Your so-called best friend clocks a discoloured bottle of ouzo, discovered by the landlord in a back-street bar in Faliraki, and orders shots. Relax, this is just a bad dream, and the reason I have still to plan my stag do.

This chapter was originally just called 'The Dreaded Top Shelf', until I realised this may allude to a certain shelf in the newsagent's, so I added a little context.

I believe the perfect pub should cater for everyone and that includes the top shelf, but please forgive me, dear reader, for taking a glossy overview rather than going into too much detail.

We have already discussed whisky and gin; next up, vodka.

Vodka

Vodka is a distilled drink whose main ingredients are ethanol and water. Traditionally, it is made by distilling cereal grains or potatoes, but technically it can be distilled from any fermentable agricultural product.

It is thought to originate from either Russia or Poland in the 14th century. The two countries are still debating who initially created the drink. My money is on a burly man with a moustache. This spirit was mainly popular in Eastern Europe. It was only after World War II that vodka's allure spread to the rest of Europe and North America. Both Edwin Starr and The Temptations asked what war is good for. A flippant answer to that question is popularising vodka and gin.

As it is a neutral spirit, the beauty of vodka is it can be mixed with a plethora of drinks to create such famous cocktails as the Bloody Mary, Cosmopolitan, Moscow Mule, Black Russian, Screwdriver, Espresso Martini and vodka Martini.

Our ventriloquist friend, Paul Zerdin, loves a vodka Martini. Paul and Leo sup away like Bond and Xenia Onatopp, the girl who crushed the admiral to death with her thighs. Call me James Bland, but it is too pokey for this guy. It looks glamorous but, to me, it's an olive floating in pure alcohol.

Leo is quite partial to a vodka, fresh lime and tonic. It is low in sugar, and arguably better for you than beer or wine.

Homemade vodka is known as moonshine. In fact, my Dad produced his own vodka called Moonshine Vodka, but alas it wasn't as big a hit as Sheep Dip and Pig's Nose. My Dad says:

> *"Vodka is not as popular in a country pub as in a town pub, but we still stock about a dozen different brands, as people do like choice."*

In our perfect pub we would stock the classics: Absolute, Smirnoff, Grey Goose, Belvedere and Stolichnaya. A locally sourced vodka, if available, would also be a nice touch.

Tequila

For a long time, in this country, tequila was seen as a celebratory drink. Perhaps it was the influence of American television and cinema, but a tequila shot was a communal dare.

There was always one person overly keen to do it, usually the sadist that ordered the round, and the rest of the group were put-upon participants.

We all know the ritual. First, you moisten the back of one hand, pour on some salt. By licking the salt, you lessen the tequila burn. Next, you slug the shot. Finally, sink your teeth into a lemon or lime wedge, not for relief, as some might think, but to enhance the flavour of the tequila.

When I did a tequila shot, I felt it was a bonding experience. Afterwards, you congratulate one another, slapping each other on the back, with sticky salty hands. My friend Charlie Offer liked the idea of beating the shot and coming through unscathed. The makes tequila sound like poison, and the salt and citrus wedge its antidote. Of course, tequila itself was not the problem, we were drinking a cheap version. Cut price wine isn't to be savoured, so why try to enjoy bad tequila?

Similar to the rules of champagne, only tequila made in Mexico can rightfully carry the name. It is made from the fermented juice of the agave plant. True tequila contains 100 per cent blue agave sugar. Mixto tequila is a sugared down version and only requires at least 51 per cent blue agave sugar; the remainder is made up of other sugar sources.

The first tequila to arrive in Britain was Mixto Tequila. Quality tequila is meant to be sipped and appreciated, rather than knocked back through gritted teeth. If you order a quality brand like Herradura Añejo Tequila, you don't even need salt or a citrus wedge for comfort. Always look for 100 per cent agave; it should be declared on the label.

Three Tequila Facts

1   Cuervo was the first tequila producer in the world. Jose Antonio de Cuervo y Valdes began production in 1758.
2   Bing Crosby is alleged to have been one of the pioneering

importers of tequila into the US. Herradura, just mentioned, was his favourite Mexican tipple, and the first 100 per cent blue agave tequila available in North America.

3   It's good for you! It lowers cholesterol levels and improves your indigestion. Imagine being prescribed Tequila by your doctor.

At the end of our first date, Leo poured me a glass of Patron Café, which is a tequila coffee liqueur. Naturally, we traded tequila experiences. She told me she had met Cleo Rocos at a party. As a childhood fan of the Kenny Everett Show, I was spellbound; when I was seven years old, my ultimate ambition was to be on that show. Leo told me Cleo Rocos was great company, and how she waxed lyrical about tequila. She even has her own brand, called Aquariva, which is 100 per cent blue agave, of course. It must be good: Britain's Tequila Society honoured her with the title of Tequila Queen of the UK.

Every 24th of July Mexicans celebrate World Tequila Day. Maybe we should celebrate this in our perfect pub. However, I do pity anyone who has a birthday on this particular date; previous toasts may have been with Mixto Tequila.

Baileys Irish Cream

The Anchor stocks about a dozen liqueurs, which sounds about right to me. My Dad informed me, "Baileys, Benedictine, and Drambuie are popular post dinner."

Whenever I think of Baileys, it reminds me of an old school friend, Rakesh Pancha. Panch, as he was known, was a powerful prop forward, from India. He had a friendly face, but when he removed his glasses, and squinted, he looked like Mike Tyson. His other distinguishing feature was a broad Bristolian accent. I thought he was teetotal, until one day he emerged from a throng at the bar with a creamy liquid in his glass, and announced "This 'ere Baileys is an orrrrgasm on the tongue!"

Rum

As an avid reader of *Treasure Island* as a child, I associate rum with the West Indies, navy, and piracy. It evokes a spirit of adventure and misadventure.

Rum is distilled from sugar cane byproducts, such as molasses or cane juice. The distillation occurs in a pot or still, before maturing in oak barrels. Rum can be made anywhere in the world, but favours areas that produce sugar cane. Rum was first distilled in the Caribbean in the 17th century, when the plantation slaves realised molasses could be fermented into alcohol.

Light rums are used in cocktails, and darker rums are drunk neat, or on the rocks. Navy rum is traditionally dark and full bodied.

One of my brothers-in-law, James Slade, used to share a flat with a guy called Hardo. He was pale, portly and always in a suit. However, he had a thick West Indian accent. He was a white Trinidadian, his accent at odds with his appearance. There was nothing funnier than to hear him describe himself as "An accountant" in a thick West Indian accent. Hardo was a huge rum drinker, and always complaining about pubs serving a poor selection. One night we were all drinking in St Paul's, the West Indian quarter of Bristol, when Hardo began holding court on the merits of rum. He had some peculiar looks from his fellow West Indian drinkers, as they thought he was mimicking their accent, while drunk.

I imagine your stock of rum would vary, depending where your perfect pub is. If you are situated near a port or on the west coast of England, you should supply a good range of rum. Young hipsters have embraced pirates, so I imagine they would be easily persuaded to drink a boatload of rum. Just beware of rum-swilling accountants from Trinidad.

Port

I have a penchant for port; it's a wonderfully smooth winter drink. At home, I will happily sup a glass on its own, but in a pub the only time I would drink port is with a cheeseboard.

Port is a Portuguese fortified wine, also known as Vinho Do Porto. It rose to prominence in England after the Methuen Treaty in 1703, which decreed that English merchants were allowed to import port at a lower duty, at a time when war with France deprived them of French wine.

It is interesting to note how tax breaks have affected alcohol consumption. In the last chapter I mentioned how William of Orange increased the tax on beer to encourage the realm to drink gin, and in Chapter 8 I mentioned it was Gordon Brown's 2002 tax breaks on small brewers which provided the platform for the craft beer revolution.

Like Champagne, the port name is tied to the region. Since 2006 only those wines made in the Douro Valley in Portugal can use the protected geographical name (those made before 2006 can still use the term). One cheeky American producer launched a fortified wine called Quady's Batch 88 Starboard Californian Port. Others followed with USB Port and Aero Port.

There are several types of port we could stock. These are the most common:

Ruby Port – the commonplace port, most of us drink. It is a youngish port, bottled after being aged for two or three years. It is also the least expensive.

Late Bottled Vintage (LBV) – originally destined to be vintage port, this batch would have been left unsold, so instead it is left in the wood barrels for four to six years before bottling. The result is lighter than vintage port, but still full of character

White Port – ranges from dry to very sweet. Young white ports are a good base for cocktails; older white ports are best served chilled and on their own.

Tawny Port – aged for between 10 and 40 years in wood barrels and bottles. A delicious non-vintage style. The older it is, the smoother and nuttier it becomes, like me!

Crusted Port – not the most glamorous name! It is far better than it sounds. This is a blend of several vintages. It is bottled early, without filtration, so it matures in the bottle. It will have a heavy sediment and should be decanted.

Vintage Port – port from a single year – and only in the best years do they 'declare' a vintage. The wines should be matured in the bottle for at least 10 years before decanting. Many are preserved in a cellar and allowed to mature for decades. I have always wanted to drink one from my birth year.

Single-Quinta Vintage Port – port from the best wine estates, but the second-best years. It should be fine, but don't mistake it for real vintage port. They are ready to drink after 10 years.

In our perfect pub we would probably stock at least one example of each type, from brands such as Taylor, Cockburn, Croft and Dow. If they sound English rather than Portuguese, this is because they were the names of the British merchant houses who shipped Port back to England.

If you are at a formal dinner it is polite to pass the port to the left, or indeed the port side. However, we are dealing with matters of the pub, so if you do order a bottle, rather than a glass, feel free to drink it as you wish.

Absinthe

Some historians allege that absinthe was first created in Switzerland in 1792 by the Henriod sisters, who used it as a herbal remedy, and that the prescribing of absinthe was pioneered by Dr Pierre Ordinaire. I love his name; it is so mismatched with the product, and yet perfect. The French make the unremarkable seem sexy. If he was English, it would not scan so well:

> "Who invented this magical potion?"
> "Peter Ordinary!"

Absinthe is an extraordinary drink. It is green in colour, and was known in Parisian artistic circles as *la fée verte*, which translates as the green fairy. That nickname makes me think of washing up liquid.

In 1859 Édouard Manet produced his famous painting 'The Absinthe Drinker', and the drink was very popular in late-19th and early-20th-century France, particularly among Parisian artists and writers. Devotees included such luminaries as van Gogh, Picasso, Hemingway, Joyce, Wilde and Proust.

By 1915 absinthe was banned in most countries, after a lengthy campaign by the Temperance Movement. In the 1990s it had a brief revival during the *Loaded* generation. Some bright spark, allegedly the entrepreneur George Rowley, realised it had never officially been banned in the UK, and began importing it from Czechoslovakia. The first time I saw absinthe for sale was in the Night and Day café bar, on Oldham Street, in Manchester.

There are several methods of preparing absinthe; the traditional French way involves a sugar cube and a special spoon. This spoon has specially designed slots, rather like a Welsh love spoon. You pour a measure of absinthe into a glass, lay the spoon over the glass, and place a sugar cube on top. Iced water is dripped over the sugar and filters through the spoon, to mix with the absinthe. The recommended ratio is one part absinthe to three to five parts water. The water brings out flavours of aniseed, fennel and star anise in the drink. Although, which absinthe drinker says:

> *"Ooh. I would never drink absinthe just to get drunk and blow*
> *my mind, I just like the flavour. Reminds me of sweeties."*

If you are thinking, hang on, I thought preparing absinthe involved fire, you are referring to the Bohemian method. This is a fairly modern innovation, and not the style used in turn of the 20th-century Paris.

Absinthe's hallucinogenic qualities are greatly exaggerated. Maybe it has become part of the myth. What I can confirm is that it is exceptionally strong in alcohol, which is said to be in the 45–74% ABV range.

I have only tasted absinthe once; it was in my early 20s, with my university friends, and it led to quite a night. It didn't taste as powerful as I expected, but there was a strong aniseed kick. That wasn't the only kick. Shortly afterwards, I remember vaulting the Seven Sisters tube gates in north London as if I was Colin Jackson. Maybe absinthe is a performance-enhancing drug for hurdlers.

I recall one of my uni friends, Cheesy Ben, who imbibed rather too much absinthe, dangling from a beam over the upper level of the Coal Hole. This is a famous old pub on the Strand, where the actor Richard Harris used to be a regular. Cheesy Ben was retrieving his shoe from a cross beam when he found himself dangling from the pub rafters, like a hapless Harold Lloyd. In a moment of drunken sincerity and desperation, I shouted down to poor Richard Harris, innocently nursing his Guinness:

> *"Hey Dumbledore! Help!"*

He was not amused, and neither was the bar manager, who asked us to leave.

Conclusion

Having discussed the dreaded top shelf, I feel I have confronted my fears. These drinks are not all evil spirits to be afraid of. The trick is to do a bit of research, spend a little more, and drink the good stuff. Still, it gives rise to some good stories.

SOFT DRINKS AND THE DESIGNATED DRIVER

15

TWO WORDS changed the pub soft drinks market overnight: drink driving.

My Dad recounted to me what life was like in the '70s – people would have a few pints and drive home. That sounds anarchic and rash, so allow me to put it into context: there were far fewer cars on the road and those cars were considerably less powerful. When has anyone said: "A Morris Minor hurtled out of nowhere."?

The worst-case scenario, back then, in my parents' village, is that someone drunk would drive off the road and plough into a ditch. From there they would walk home, or abandon all hope and head back to the pub. Once back at base camp they would be greeted with ridicule, given a conciliatory pint, or a coffee, and a farmer would offer to tow them out with a tractor in the morning. Those were simpler times. Nowadays, almost everyone has a car and those cars are powerful death machines. Drinking and driving is lethal and not to be condoned, even if you are a professional footballer.

If you want to know what life was like in the '70s, travel to rural Ireland. That isn't a diss. Life is simpler and unspoilt on the West Coast of Ireland. I mentioned visiting a pub called O'Looneys in Chapter 10. When we left the pub, at around 1am, the barman said:

"Are you walking home or driving?"
ME: *"We're walking."*
BARTENDER: *"Why don't you drive home? It's a lot safer.*
   Be careful though. There's drunk drivers all over town."
ME: *"Ha! I can almost see the logic, but we'll still waddle."*

In Ireland, they have an overtaking lane, so there is an extra line, like a hard shoulder, on the road. Some of the locals, allegedly, use it as a line to follow when driving back from the pub. We decided to do the right thing and walk. However when we got back to our camp, we found our tent had blown against a barbed wire fence and was ripped to sheds. We had to pick out our backpacks from amongst the dayglo debris, trudge back to the pub and sleep in our car. Addendum to don't drink and drive: don't drink and camp. What a bizarre turn of events; if we weren't so relaxed, we'd have 'craic-ed' under the pressure.

How Drink Driving Affected Our Village Pub

Running a village pub, a short drive from the nearest town, meant that my Dad's business was shaken by the drink driving laws. But like Hannibal from the A-Team, he had a plan that would come together. The germ of the idea sprouted while waiting for a delayed flight at Gatwick Airport, where he spied a cart selling freshly squeezed orange juice. Instantly, he knew it was the way forward. My Dad had tried to make orange juice before, albeit an alcoholic orange juice. He mixed cider with orange juice and called it 'Saravana'. I remember these dusty brown bottles, very '70s. They would be well camouflaged if left on an orange and brown shag-pile carpet.

I was a bit hazy on a few precise details on the origins of his orange juice, so I consulted my Dad, over a cup of tea in his conservatory. I plonked my iPhone on the table and interviewed him, Parkinson style. He was far from apprehensive, launched straight in, and we ended up with 45 minutes of recorded footage. Half-way through my Mum tiptoed in, as I think she thought it was a live recording rather than a brainstorming session. She asked whether it was being recorded for Radio 4.

Bless her! How delightfully supportive is she? My influence isn't that great. To be fair, the previous month I had recorded a piece about the perfect pub for Radio 4, on my iPhone, and e-mailed it to the studio, but that was a one-off.

Soft Drinks as Mixers in the '70s and '80s

I interviewed my Dad on his thoughts about soft drinks and he unearthed the following nuggets:

> *"In the old days fizzy drinks were aimed at children.*
> *They were also used as mixers in drinks like gin and tonic,*
> *whisky and dry ginger, gin and orange and (pause for effect)*
> *… Snowballs!"*
> ME: *"What's a Snowball?"*
> DAD: *"Advocaat and lemonade."*
> ME: *"Ew! Sounds more like yellow snow."*
> DAD: *"People came back from Spain and wanted Cuba Libres,*
> *which was white rum and Coca Cola."*
> ME: *"A Cuba Libre certainly sounds a lot flashier than just*
> *rum and coke."*
> DAD: *"There was a lot of lemonade used in shandies.*
> *But most soft drinks were for the kids."*

It's strange to think that in the current climate, where some folk are watching their alcohol intake, there isn't more shandy being drunk. Even the word shandy sounds really old fashioned. In our local store, among the soft drinks in the fridge, there is always a can of Shandy Bass, the blue can with the little red triangle. Maybe it was left there from the 1980s, or stuck to the shelf like one of those joke 50p pieces you find superglued to the bar top.

> DAD: *"There is a large proportion of people who don't drink,*
> *but want a healthy drink."*

Nowadays you have initiatives such as Dry January and Sober October. I have to admit, not only have I not tried these detox plans, last January I actually contracted gout. I know. What year is this? Pass me an orange, I need to ward off scurvy.

There are exceptions. My friend Mark Olver, a talented compere and king of the television warm-up, is teetotal but loves visiting pubs. The last time we gigged together, he showed me a super cool craft beer bar in the back streets of Nottingham called Kean's Head. I say the back streets, but it is situated in the Lace Market, which is hardly The Bronx. I digress. I supped a pint of Harvest Pale, from Castle Rock Brewery, while Mark ordered a pie and chugged contentedly on a pint of Diet Coke.

At Kean's Head, Nottingham

Frobishers Fruit Juice

My Dad and his best friend, Ian McDonald, created a range of freshly pressed juices and launched it in 1992. They chose the name Frobishers because they did not fancy using their own surnames and it sounds healthy, rural and home made. It began as a family operation. I remember, after dinner, our family would gather round and form a production line to put labels on the bottles, build the cardboard trays and shrink-wrap the batch.

I recall sitting at the dinner table, when I was about 12, and my Dad asking the family to come up with a marketing slogan for Frobishers. Through a mouthful of faggots, mash and peas, I gurgled the suggestion:

"The fruit, the whole fruit and nothing but the fruit."

This strapline lasted for 15 years. I should have negotiated some residual payments, or at least an advance in pocket money. Still, it was good to wear a T-shirt with my own slogan emblazoned on the front.

DAD: *"I started Frobishers as I could see a gap in the market. Most fruit juices were made from juice concentrate and served in small 4oz baby bottles. They were incredibly cheap. When we first launched Frobishers Juices we brought them out in a 250ml serve and publicans couldn't see the sense, as they could buy concentrate at 5p a bottle, whereas Frobishers was around 50p per bottle cost price."*

"Eventually the quality shone through. Wherever we distributed beer [my Dad also ran a beer distribution business] we would leave a few bottles of complimentary Frobishers for the bar staff. They would tell the landlord they liked them and an order was put in."

I know I'm biased, but that's good business strategy.

DAD: *"The idea of Frobishers fruit juice came from the fact that I have been partly responsible for the distribution of draught beer, which I felt was a natural product. We wanted to do the same for fruit juice as we did for beer. What most people don't realise is that most fruit juices are made from concentrated juice, or they were in those days [the 1990s]. The concentrate arrives in the UK and you let one part down with six parts of water..."*

ME: *"Like orange squash?"*

DAD: *"Yes. That's right. So the water which the oranges grew with in South America is a different water to the one it is let down with so, to me, it is not a natural product. Whereas we would import the actual oranges into the UK and we would squeeze them ourselves, giving a more natural product. We then took the juice up to a certain temperature, which destroyed any potential bugs in it. The selling point was that Frobishers was a freshly pressed juice with a 12- month shelf life."*

Concentrated juice has a much shorter shelf life, and needs to be consumed quickly or else it goes off, whereas a juice with a 12-month shelf life is much more attractive to the licensing trade.

Decline of Lunchtime Drinking

My Dad also made a final point that had not occurred to me:

"Lunchtime drinking in pubs has decreased dramatically, as office workers aren't allowed to drink if they have to use a computer."

I thought it was just heavy machinery we had to steer clear of after a boozy lunch. My Dad isn't that computer literate, so maybe he is imagining a retro PC desktop computer, the size of a washing machine, with warning signs in the office saying 'Don't drink and type.'

Our Perfect Range

I would say that, even 20 years ago, there was slim pickings when it came to a choice of soft drinks, just Coca Cola, lemonade, orange juice, tonic water, squash or lime and soda.

I have to conclude that non-alcoholic drinks are now much more important to a pub than they were 30 years ago. We need a range of good-quality freshly pressed juices and some cheaper options. Those include having a jug of tap water at the end of the bar, maybe even cucumber-infused tap water for the trendy folk. Leo's current favourite non-alcoholic drink is Belvoir Elderflower Pressé. Served with ice, it is beautifully refreshing. Luscombe also produce a delicious version. I believe soda water should be free and a mixer, for example, a shot of lime, no more than 40p. Anything higher is daylight robbery.

Soft Drink Dispenser Gun

I am referring to the multi-function button-operated single nozzle soft drink dispensing hosepipe. That is a mouthful. The contraption is called many different names, but I am going with this.

I believe the Soft Drink Dispenser, with its all-encompassing Swiss army nozzle, is a utensil we can do without. How many times have you ordered a soft drink, only to find the syrup mix is out of whack, and your cola is too weak or too syrupy? Both are bad. Put the gun down. If you want a fizzy drink, have it poured from the bottle.

Coffee

Finally, I like the Wetherspoon's model of offering a mug of Lavazza coffee for 99p. They even provide free filter coffee refills before 2pm. My favourite part of that sentence is 'before 2pm', as if that is the cut off point:

> *"Come on folks, it's 2pm, we are embracing the afternoon, your hangovers should be yesterdays' news, time to stroke the hair of the dog."*

There is a good profit to be had in coffee, but it should be straightforward to make. There is nothing worse than a queue forming at the bar because someone ordered a batch of coffees. So, if you have to, get them in before 2pm.

Reading this chapter back, I realise I have delegated most of the soft drinks section to my Dad. Let's just say I was appealing to my resident expert, rather admitting the only soft drinks I consume are tap water, tea and coffee. No wonder I have gout!

BEER MONSTER MUNCHIES

DRINKING BOOZE gives us the munchies, and after a few beverages there is nothing like a good pub snack to hit the spot.

Sharing Crisps in the Pub

Allegedly, Walkers increased the size of their crisp bag from the regular 32.5g to the 50g grab bag, purely for people to share in the pub. It was estimated if you offered a crisp to all your friends, you'd still be able to enjoy the traditional amount yourself. Intriguing fact though that is, there is a certain method we use when opening crisps in a pub. We don't tear it open at the top and proffer to pals to dip their paws in; this isn't a school playground. We unzip the seam of the bag and let it cascade down slowly like a little black dress. Sound saucy? Of course it does. I love crisps.

One Flavour

This might sound crazy, but in the mid- to late-'80s my Dad only stocked one flavour of crisps: plain.

There was some method in his madness. Families or large groups had a tendency to approach the bar for some crisps and ask what flavours were on offer. The bartender would list all the flavours. Some folks decided on their flavour straightaway, but others memorised them and popped to their table to find out everyone's preference, before returning to make their order. All this time the bartender was kept waiting. This whole charade wasted precious minutes, while wild-eyed farmers and fishermen grumpily waited their turn to recharge their glasses. My Dad maintained the amount of beer you could pour went up under his communist one-crisp rule. But like most communist ideals, it didn't last.

History of the Potato Crisp

The potato crisp may have originated in North America on 24 August 1853, in Saratoga Springs, New York. Legend has it that the invention of the crisp was a happy accident. A fussy customer, the gloriously named Cornelius Vanderbilt, complained to a chef called Crum (cracking name for a chef), that his potatoes were sliced too thick. In a fit of pique, Crum sliced the spuds razor thin, cooked them to a crisp and added far too much salt. To Crum's surprise, they were a big hit and became known as Saratoga Chips.

In the UK, Frank Smith, an apprentice greengrocer, was instrumental in popularising crisps. According to Steve Berry and Phil Norman, authors of *A Brief History of Crisps*:

> '*Noticing his boss's sideline of frying up a few bags of potato crisps as a novelty for his customers, he took over the operation and expanded it, selling to other shops and especially pubs, where brewers welcomed their lucrative powers of dehydration. By 1913 he was turning out 1,000 bags a week, and in 1920, after he opened a dedicated factory in a disused Cricklewood garage, that figure rose to half a million.*'

The UK naturally embraced the crisp. Frank Smith had popped in a twist of salt in greaseproof paper bags, but no one thought to add any further flavour until the 1950s when Joe 'Spud' Murphy, owner of Tayto, developed a flavouring technique. The first three flavours were Cheese & Onion, Barbecue, and Salt & Vinegar. Amazing to think that two out of three of those are still the most popular flavours today. Barbecue surprises me; I did not expect it to be one of the original flavours. As this was post-war, I'd have put my money on Tripe and Onion, Spam Fritter or Beef Dripping.

1980s Crisps

When I started drinking in pubs in the early '90s, Walkers and Smith's crisps seemed to be the pub crisps of choice, ably supported by Bacon and Scampi fries. When did it become all about Kettle Chips? They market themselves as a healthier option, but after five pints you're not looking for a health kick. Some kettle chips feel like you're chewing through potpourri.

Walkers now have 56% of the UK market. I recently avoided Walkers in attempt to support smaller brands like Quavers, Frazzles and Square Crisps. However, a bit of research reveals that all these crisps are owned by Walkers and they in turn are under the same multinational parent company, Pepsi. So, technically, you can do the Pepsi Challenge with crisps.

One of my potential Dragon's Den-type ideas would be a vending machine stocking old school snacks. It means people can take their time over picking their crisps, without holding up the bar staff.

What would I stock in my vending machine? Well, one flavour you don't often see in pubs these days, but is an absolute doozy, is Brannigan's Ham and Mustard. They have a powerful flavour, which cuts through a good strong autumnal ale like Hobgoblin or Tanglefoot. In that respect they may be described as a winter crisp. Monster Munch, Wotsits and Space Raiders are rare in pubs, as they may be considered childish, but after a few drinks most of us regress to a child-like state anyway, so what's the problem? Leo and I are currently crushing on Bacon Streaks, which are less salty than a Frazzle, and cheaper.

The oddest crisp combo I've seen was back home, where some of the locals like a pickled egg in a packet of salt and vinegar. You drop it in and give it shake, like a West Country Jägerbomb snack. It tastes nicer than it sounds.

Pork Scratchings

Pork scratchings were singled out a few times as vital ingredients in the perfect pub over the course of my Edinburgh stand-up run. Interestingly, always by men. I think they may taste best with a hearty ale. Dogs will eat them with anything. I assumed pork scratchings are bad for you. To me, they are just fat but, apparently, they qualify as a superfood for athletes. Wow! My flabber is well and truly gasted. According to *Men's Health* magazine, a 1oz (28g) serving of pork scratchings contains nine times the protein and less fat than a packet of crisps, which are much higher in carbohydrates. So, the next time you pop open a packet, tell people you're in training.

Nuts

Peanuts are a must. At school I was nicknamed 'Peanut', as my mate Si once charmingly suggested my head was shaped like a peanut. I love peanuts and could happily live on dry-roasted. I must stress I'm talking about packet peanuts, not bar peanuts; the less said about them the better.

The peanut is referred to as a nut for simplicity, but it is actually classified as both a grain and a legume. There you go, pub quiz fans. They are grow in pods beneath the soil. Forty six million tonnes of peanuts are produced each year and 37% of those are from China.

KP nuts are ubiquitous in pubs. KP – originally Kenyon Produce – started selling nuts in 1952, beginning with roasted salted hazelnuts, as they were the only nuts available. Once the peanut reared its peanut-shaped head there was no looking back.

Nobby's Nuts are originally from Australia. Who else but the Aussies would take the peanut and try and make it more blokey?

Pistachios are a delight. Even the art of shelling them is moreish. After a few ales, I often forget and munch the shells as well, a sight that confounds and astonishes poor Leo.

Salted cashews are delicious and come with various sprinkles of flavouring. My sister Talia started a company called Talia's Nuts, which always tickled me. She made and sold her own recipe of spiced cashews to pubs in the West Country, and I was a self-appointed taste tester. Add that to Pub Scout and Cheese Counsellor and I'm building quite the left-field c.v.

If you like spice and a little kick, look no further than Wasabi peas or, as I call them, 'the greens that are fun to eat'. I often forget how peppery they are, pop a handful in my mouth, recoil in surprise, gasp for breath and repeat the same process a few minutes later.

Pastries

Sausage rolls, especially gourmet ones, are delicious with a dollop of ketchup. They are a regular fixture in the Antic chain of pubs in London.

A good Scotch egg is delectable. The best I've ever eaten was in the Catford Constitutional Club, in south-east London. Again, another from the Antic chain. The pork layer seemed better quality than the usual Scotch egg, and the egg inside was slightly runny. I am salivating just thinking about it. As Leo would say, "Yumbo!"

Olives

Olives are a very inviting bar snack. I like my olives fleshy, green and pitted. Our friend Paul Zerdin introduced us to Perelló pitted olives, which are a firm, yet pulpy delicacy. They originate from Andalusia, in Spain and their full title is Perelló Gordal Pitted Green Olives Picante. The word 'Gordal' translates as 'the fat one' in Spanish, which is just what you wish for in an olive. The marinade contains a gentle kick of Guindilla chilli. We order them from Amazon, but they are available in a few delicatessens. Do not skimp on the quality of olives; average olives are a waste of time.

Cockles

Finally, who can forget the fish man who would waddle in with a tray of whelks, cockles and jellied eels, like a human embodiment of a Chas & Dave song. I've never bought any. To me, it seems at odds with the surroundings, like setting up a hot dog stand in a library.

Our Snack Selection

Our perfect pub would offer a wide variety of crisps, and would be happy to stock any other flavours requested by regular customers. I would have a mainstream nuts brand and some locally sourced. Jars of Perelló pitted olives would be on hand, so too good-quality home-made sausage rolls, which never go cold, and never run out. If this smorgasbord of snacks does not satisfy your cravings, check out my 'old school' vending machine in the corner.

FOOD, GLORIOUS PUB FOOD

17

BORN AND BRAISED in a pub, I have probably dined on pub food more than most.

Good-quality pub food and the rise of the gastro-pub are fairly recent phenomena. In the old days you ate at home and drank in the pub; now it's the other way round.

I was intrigued by George Orwell's thoughts on pub food back in 1946:

> 'You cannot get dinner at the Moon Under Water, but there is always the snack counter where you can get liver-sausage sandwiches, mussels (a speciality of the house), cheese, pickles and those large biscuits with caraway seeds in them which only seem to exist in public-houses. Upstairs, six days a week, you can get a good, solid lunch – for example, a cut off the joint, two vegetables and boiled jam roll – for about three shillings.'

I love mussels and am enthralled at the idea that Orwell considers them a pub snack. Bring on the snacks, I say. The 'liver sausage sandwich' seems like a precursor to the modern hot dog; and cheese, pickle and biscuits has certainly stood the test of time. A lunch of meat and two veg, with a pudding, although unimaginative, provides solid sustenance.

Some pubs have a long association with providing food and victuals, dating back to their role as an inn for travellers to rest their weary and thirsty heads. In the 1950s some pubs offered a simple pie and a pint.

Ploughman's Lunch

In the 1960s it became popular to lunch as the ploughmen do. They were obviously the celebrity eaters of the age. Despite this, potential TV shows such as 'Ploughmen vs. Food' and 'The Great British Plough Off' have yet to materialise. Still, their midday snack of cheese and pickle with a hunk of bread was the order of the day.

According to legend, The Ploughman's Lunch was an invention of the Cheese Council to shift more cheese. I know what you're thinking: Cheese Council, there's an organisation to get your teeth into. I would love the title: 'James Dowdeswell – Cheese Councillor'. It would be an idyllic second revenue stream after 'Pub Scout'.

In the 1970s there weren't many restaurants and those that were around, like the Berni Inn and Beefeater chain (the latter suggests vegetarianism was an alien concept), sold simple fare like a prawn cocktail to start, steak and chips for main, and a black forest gateau for desert.

West Country Tapas

In the mid-'70s my Dad had a problem; people kept leaving his pub to pop home for their dinner. This was bad for business. While on holiday in Palma he watched the locals eating and drinking at tavernas and resolved to introduce his own brand of West Country tapas. Suddenly, there were Polish sausages and salami hanging from his ceiling, by the bar, like *jamon* in a Spanish taverna.

I imagine he opted for a Spanish influence, rather than Italian, because it is a West Country pub and the Italians are 'antipasti'. What's wrong with pasties? (Excuse the painful pun, but I really couldn't resist it.)

West Country tapas consisted of home-made, locally baked bread, served with a choice of: rare beef, home-made pâté, coleslaw, potato salad, sweet pickles, pickled onion and pickled eggs. All the pickles. They were stored in jars behind the bar. My Mum recalled:

'It was said, if the women ate pickled eggs, they became pregnant!'

What an aphrodisiac. No oysters required. Was I a pickled egg baby I wonder?

Finally, there was a choice of three cheeses: cheddar, double Gloucester or brie.

It was cold food only. The Anchor didn't have a kitchen back then; all the food was served from behind the bar – Orwell would have approved. It was very simple and very successful. More importantly, it achieved my father's primary objective, that of keeping the customers drinking in his pub without popping home for their dinner.

I am writing this chapter whilst gigging away at the Glee Club, Cardiff. The previous night, the comedian David Morgan was tickled pink by my Dad's Palma story and tried to order West Country tapas at a restaurant for lunch. The waiter politely reminded him he was in Wales.

1970s and 1980s Pub Food

The microwave was first sold in 1946 and developed using radar technology developed during World War II. It was originally called the 'radarange'.

There is wonderful myth that the Welsh call it 'Popty Ping'. The real Welsh word, meicrodon, is often said to sound like a small Mafia boss.

Microwaves became popular in the mid-1970s to early-1980s. The result was that food could be pre-prepared and reheated to order. Sounds bleak, but back then we didn't know any different.

Traditional pub food, right up until the late '80s, was fairly basic, and often centred around chips, which were served with any of the following: ham and egg, chicken and bacon,

177

fish, scampi, gammon, steak, or 'Surf 'n' Turf' – if you wished to mix seafood and red meat. Frying that many chips, the smoke alarm must have been on red alert.

Perhaps more controversial than his decision to only offer one flavour of crisps, my Dad refused to serve chips in his pub. He offered most other potato styles: potato salad, new potatoes, mashed, roasted, and dauphinoise. The reason being, he felt the smell of the chip fat pervaded the pub, and having worked in a fish and chip shop as a youth, was jaded by the stench.

The 1970s and 1980s was also home to a plethora of pies: pork, cottage, shepherd's, steak and kidney, steak and ale and, one of my favourites, toad in the hole. There was also comfort food like lasagne, spaghetti Bolognese and sausage and mash.

For an exotic palette there was Indian curry, especially the UK's favourite, chicken tikka masala. Its origins are murky. Some say it is Indian dish, invented for the UK, with masala sauce added to quell the British hunger for gravy. However, a Glasgow chef, Ahmed Aslam Ali, claims to have invented the dish at his Shish Mahal restaurant in Glasgow in the early '70s. Delhi's leading food historians have dismissed his claim. I imagine it is the equivalent of claiming to invent the deep-fried Mars bar in Mumbai.

Finally, a firm lunch favourite: various flavours of quiche. When I worked at Waterstone's bookshop, I used to love helping with events and book signings. After the first one, my parents asked how it went. I replied:

> *"It was fantastic. I met Stephen Fry and we*
> *had several different types of quiche."*

I was in culinary and literary heaven.

Gastro-pubs

Since the 1990s there has been more focus on pub food, with some pubs offering a separate dining room for larger parties.

The term 'gastro-pub' was first coined in 1991, when The Eagle, in Farringdon, London, decided to go gourmet and provide fine dining in a pub.

The owners, Michael Belben and David Eyre, were restaurateurs who wanted to open their own restaurant, but the London rents were too high. However, it was now easier to obtain a pub licence, so why not combine the two? Besides which, a restaurant requires a certain level of fixtures and fittings, whereas pubgoers are less fussy about decor and the sense of occasion. Eyre was quoted as saying:

> "I am always and continually bemused as to
> why The Eagle was regarded as a radical idea.
> We took an obvious idea and gave it a twist."

I like The Eagle's mantra 'Never forget it's a pub', which means the menu is blackboard-based and the seating unreserved.

My parents' pub now has a modern gastro-style dining room, but it is tucked away out the back and does not detract from the traditional rural feel of the pub.

Gastro-pubs were big business in the early Noughties. By 2003, there were 5,000 gastro-pubs in the UK. That translates as just under 10 per cent of all pubs. However, by 2011 the tide had turned and *The Good Food Guide* announced it would no longer being using the term gastro-pub. Editor of the guide, Elizabeth Carter, stated:

> 'Our feeling with the gastro-pub was that it was a bit of a
> bandwagon that a lot people have jumped on to. I think
> customers are getting bored with it. Pubs have to be socially
> diverse, they have to offer many things, whether you pop in
> for a drink and a snack or you want a proper meal.'

The gastro bubble popped and after dabbling with decadence, pubs reverted to their original priorities. Carter confirms:

*'Pubs realise that your local business is very important,
as is hospitality. It's getting away from being like
a restaurant and going back to being a pub.'*

The term gastro-pub might have gone, but the food scene in pubs has never been better and healthier.

Celebrity Pub Chefs

Some celebrity chefs emerged phoenix-like from the media flamed gastro-pubs, Heston Blumenthal for one. I love his name; say it loud and it could be a middle-class swear word!

Heston owns three establishments in Bray. He bought The Fat Duck in 1995; it was originally a run-down pub called The Ringers, which he transformed into a three-Michelin-star restaurant. In 2004 he added The Hind's Head, a gastro-pub, which also earned a Michelin star. Finally, he purchased The Crown, which he kept as a traditional pub, in 2010.

Heston seems to have a monopoly on Berkshire. With three public houses already, surely it's time to pop a hotel on, or maybe he's waiting to collect all four stations first. I must point out that Heston Service Station is nothing to do with him. Imagine glugging an amuse-bouche while filling up with petrol, although the dry ice might panic fellow customers.

Tom Kerridge is currently a popular TV chef, with an infectious enthusiasm and a delightful West Country burr. He made his name as a magnificent restaurant and pub chef. He transformed The Hand & Flowers pub into a gastro-pub extraordinaire, in 2005, and within a year of its opening, earned a Michelin star. In 2012 he scored a second, the first pub to ever do so. Since then he has come to prominence as a TV presenter, presenting *Food and Drink* on BBC. He has also published many books; I can heartily recommend his *Proper Pub Food Cookbook*, in which he says:

'For me, really great pub food should be accessible to everyone without having to compromise on standards. It should offer

value for money – notice I haven't said necessarily always
cheap, but it certainly means value for what you are eating.'

At the time of writing there are now 15 Michelin star pubs in the UK. I particularly like the sound of The Pony and Trap in Chew Magna. Good job that's in Somerset and not East London. Our cockney friends would have a field day with the rhyming slang.

Delia Smith, however is not a fan of fine pub dining. In 2011, she declared:

'On the whole… I like the '70s the best really.
Gifted amateurs opened restaurants and pubs
and where you could have real food.'

She went on to explain:

'If I am in a Michelin-starred restaurant and they have
done this beautiful little smoked haddock soufflé in
a thimble, I would like to order a whole big plateful.
No, I'm not for four-course tasting menus.'

Not quite 'Let's be having you', but certainly a call to culinary arms. Delia need not worry, it's not all gastro-pub fare. A few '70s dishes have survived: sausage and mash and steak and ale pies are a staple on most pub menus. I like to think Delia still approves of Tom Kerridge's accessibility and value ethos though.

Pub Roasts

The smoking ban and relaxed Sunday opening hours mean the pub is a great place to have Sunday lunch, and the chefs have plenty of time to prepare it. Sundays have become the busiest day of the week for a lot of pubs.

I love a good pub roast in winter. There is nothing like a good Yorkshire pudding drowning in thick onion gravy. I am salivating just thinking about it.

The secret of a good pub roast is to eat fairly early. That way you seem to get a better cut of meat. I tend to oscillate between roast beef and roast pork. I love Yorkshire pudding and insist of having it with pork too. When I was a kid I thought it was an actual pudding, and imagined it as a cake covered in chocolate sauce! I like a good selection of seasonal vegetables. It is important they are crisp and slightly *al dente*. There is no point boiling the goodness out of them; this is not school dinners.

Fancy a simple roast on the road? You cannot beat a Toby Carvery. It is a glutton's delight; not so much an all-you-can-eat, more an all-you-can-balance-on-your-plate, restaurant. I imagine circus performers are barred. I am the regular MC at a theatre in Braintree and part of my pre-gig ritual is calling in at the Carvery, around the corner. I daydream about it while sitting in the habitual hell of Friday night traffic. Sitting alone in a Carvery probably looks a little sad to the onlooker, but I am happy as a pig in a blanket. The busiest Toby Carvery I have ever ventured into was in Leeds city centre. The place was teeming on a Friday night; more big plate night than date night.

The Beefburger and Street Food in Pubs

Most pubs have now embraced the beefburger. In December 2007 Tom Byng opened the first posh burger joint, in West London. Making gourmet burgers soon became an art form. I like mine with locally sourced meat, tangy cheese, and a good-quality bun.

In 2009 burger aficionado Yianni Papoutsis popped up in South London, with a burger van and a twitter account. Word of mouth of his juicy American street burgers went viral with the hashtag #MEATWagon. I remember friends making pilgrimages south of the river to find the meat van, parked in Peckham. In late 2010, poor Yianni had his van stolen. It turned out to be a blessing in disguise. Pub owner Scott Collins offered him a pop-up burger residency in his pub, The Goldsmith's Tavern, in New Cross. They called it 'MEATeasy'. Collins and Yianni have since opened their 'MEATliquor' chain together which, at the time of writing, has 13 restaurants. The dirty burger is here to stay, and is great for soaking up the booze.

There is a growing trend of providing street food in pubs. Mini burgers are served on a tray as sliders. Pulled pork has become ubiquitous, along with Mac 'n' Cheese. Artisan pizzas, wraps, and hot dogs are also very popular. Some city pubs now regularly invite pop-up, or street, chefs into their kitchens, for short residencies. Although MEATwagons' residency was done out of necessity, they have shown what is possible.

Outsourcing

One pub I used to frequent, The Shakespeare in Stoke Newington, East London, didn't have a kitchen, so did a deal with the pizza parlour next door. That is inspired outsourcing and embraces the community vibe. That way, the businesses complement each other; they both do what they do best and everyone is happy.

I would occasionally say: "I like traditional British pub food – Thai."

Up the hill from me is a wonderful pub called Skehans. It is an Irish pub with a Thai Restaurant in the garden. I have never actually eaten in the restaurant and always order my food to be consumed in the pub. I highly recommend the chicken Massaman curry, which is to die for, especially after a few pints.

The Rise of Vegetarian and Vegan

There was a time when the vegetarian option was merely a salad, or a cheese sandwich, and a vegetarian roast was the same dish without the meat. Now, times have changed.

According to a survey conducted by Comparethemarket.com, published in April 2018, 7 million people identified with being vegetarian and 3.5 million with veganism.

Veganism has soared in the last few years, thanks to enlightening documentaries, and endorsements from such celebrities as Natalie Portman, Woody Harrelson, and Ellen DeGeneres. Sports stars such as the boxer David Haye and Arsenal footballer Hector Bellerin have also converted.

There has been a huge rise in free-from products, whether it be meat-free, gluten-free, or lactose-free. Supermarkets are catering for people with allergies and pubs should too. We want someone with allergies, or a different diet, to feel welcome, and be able to eat and drink at the pub, without worrying there won't be anything for them.

Another group, known as meat reducers, are cutting down on meat for health reasons and hoping to reduce their carbon footprint. Some meat eaters also choose a vegetarian dish because they have a hankering for something lighter or more healthy. Hearty superfood salads are also in vogue now.

Plenty of restaurant guides, including the More Than Carrots website, help people find veggie venues. If you want your pub to survive, your menu needs to include a few free-from dishes.

Conclusion

Modern city pubs now compete with chain restaurants and coffee shops. The street-food scene marries with the urban pub perfectly. The vibrant and variant nature of the current foodie wave can only enhance the pub experience.

Meanwhile, the country pub, although providing mostly more rural and traditional food, is still capable of surprises, especially in the Berkshire area.

As for gastro-pubs, the term always made me chuckle, as the word gastro in Australia is an abbreviation of gastroenteritis.

CUSTOMER SERVICE AND THE ART OF BARTENDING

18

THE ANCHOR is a lively West Country pub, especially when my father presides behind the bar. He is a natural-born landlord, with a booming voice, and likes to speak from the diaphragm, like Brian Blessed on hearing good news about Flash Gordon. I call it his Beer-itone voice.

My Dad's pint glass is always half full and bottomless. Maybe his glass is bi-focal, and looks bigger at the bottom. Whatever the reason, it is refreshing to see someone radiate such positivity in this cynical modern world.

One of my favourite facts about my father is that he claims never to have called "Last orders", as he thinks it is negative and bad for business. He prefers phrases like, "Next orders" and "Further requirements." However, it was the unique way in which he called last orders that became his party piece.

We've been out drinking in Bristol, on more than one occasion, when other landlords have requested he step in and call time in their pubs. Most landlords give a brass bell a tinkle and enquire whether people actually have homes to go to, whereas my Dad gives a flamboyant performance. He treats his customers to the full pomp and ceremony. He would plant his feet shoulder-width apart, strike his opening note "Maaaaaaay..." and hold it until puce in the face. The whole bar stops. Just before his face turns purple, he follows up with:

"...aaaay we have your next orders ladies and gentlemen."

Finally as steam whistles from his ears, he hits the high note, "Pleeeeeeeeeease!" It's dramatic, almost operatic and keeps the pub party in full swing.

All the Bar's a Stage

The comedian, Russell Howard, used to live in a neighbouring village, and his parents popped in The Anchor fairly regularly. One day Russell's Dad, Dave, approached the bar and said to my father:

> DAVE: *"Mike, you're a businessman, what do you make of our sons, eschewing proper jobs to do this standing up comedy?"*

> DAD: *"Well, I don't know about you Dave, but I view my son performing comedy as mere practice for the real stage..."*

My father swept his arm across his body, theatrically:

"...behind the bar!"

To be honest, Russell and I should never be put behind the same bar. Imagine trying to get served by two easily distracted bartenders, with lazy eyes. It would be carnage. Send in the clowns!

My Parents Behind the Bar

Running a good bar is much harder than it looks, and like many people who have mastered a skill, they make it look easy. Some customers saw my parents having fun behind the bar and thought they'd give it a whirl. Those publicans never lasted.

My parents are more than a team; they are a great double-act. Their stage was behind the bar. They dressed up, had fun and put on a show. Their motto is "When you go out, shine."

Their styles complemented each other: my Dad is a showman, my Mum, the straight act.

I interviewed them both to find out the most important bartending skills they had acquired over the years:

MUM: *"You must have a sense of humour behind the bar. You have to be fun and be able to laugh at yourself as well. And have the ability to take the mickey out of the customers, without upsetting them."*

DAD (warming to the subject): *"Do you know, you've got it in one, an ability to deliver abuse to the regulars without causing offence."*

MUM: *"I only had to drop a glass and someone would say 'Is Jenny in the building?' They still say it now, and I haven't worked there for 20 years!"*

'Cheers' – "Where Everyone Knows Your Name"

Like the fictional Boston bar in the sitcom *Cheers*, my folks are known for remembering everyone's names. The customers are always impressed with this. Their method is to remember the name alongside one key fact. Someone will pop in for the first time in five years and they'll be greeted with:

"Hi Keith, how are the goats?"
*"Welcome Jamie Hogg, best centre-half I've ever seen.
 What are you drinking?"*
"Bernard, how's the crossword today?"

Very occasionally they would forget a name. I remember having lunch with my Mum and sister when the phone rang. It was my Dad, calling from the pub:

*"Jenny, what's the name of the chap who drives the cherry red
 Volkswagen Beetle?"*

When they presided behind the bar together, they had to be sneakier. So they would duck down behind the bar, where there was a ground-level gravity-fed beer tap, and collude, while pretending to pour a pint.

My Dad specialised in recalling all the adult names; my Mum's domain was babies and dogs, which went down equally well.

George Orwell would certainly concur. In his 'Moon Under Water' essay, he wrote:

> 'The barmaids know most of their customers by name,
> and take a personal interest in everyone.'

As a brief caveat, I must stipulate that I do appreciate that using a customer's name is much easier in a country pub. In a city or town pub there might only be handful of regulars. Trying to recall all the names in an inner-city pub may come across as a little over-familiar. Today's bar staff may also have to double-up as waiters. So the type of individualised attention Orwell hoped for isn't always possible. However, when you do find it, it's precious.

Six Qualities in Good Bartending, According to My Parents

Aside from the qualities already mentioned, here are my parents' top bartending tips:

1   DAD: "The most important thing for bar staff is a smile on their face. A big smile, a genuine smile, works wonders. This should be followed by a warm greeting the moment a customer arrives, preferably within five seconds."

2   DAD: "Clear and concise delivery of drinks and food. Precise instructions of how long it will be and asking where they would like to sit, etc."

3   MUM: "If there are any complaints, dealing with them calmly and sensibly."

4   DAD: "Feedback from the customers is very important and should be dealt with straight away."

5   MUM: "When you're really busy, acknowledge a new customer, even if you're not ready to serve them, e.g. 'Be with you in a minute sir/madam.'"

6   DAD: "Also, if the bartender is telling a story while they are serving, it must be addressed to everyone and not just one person. People get upset if, while being served, the bartender is talking to someone else."

My Bartending Experience

When I was a student at Swansea University I was a regular in The Woodman, a wonderful pub at the foot of Clyne Gardens, near The Mumbles. At the end of the first year the landlord, Darren, took me aside and said:

> "James, you spend most of your time in my pub.
> How would you like to work here?
> You'll be here anyway, only now you'll get paid."

It was the only time in my life I have been headhunted! I phoned my parents for advice:

ME: *"What makes a good bartender?"*
DAD: *"A person who can do five things at once and*
    talk to five different customers at once."
ME: *"Multi-tasking? Uh-oh! Better strap in."*

Darren, the manager of The Woodman, was a great teacher. He was a young Australian, with long curly hair, tied back in a ponytail. He wore black trousers, white shirt and a black bow tie. He insisted we wore the same. It was the only time at university that I looked smart.

The locals used to come in, flirt with a barmaid, hurl abuse at me, and get served by Darren. I was essentially a stooge, but it was a good team effort.

Gradually, the locals warmed to me. Darren entrusted me to keep to look after them and keep their glasses topped up. If their pint was empty, I was to serve them straightaway, and take the money when the moment should arise.

The first time locals took me out on the town, I didn't have time to change out of my tuxedo. We went to some incredibly rough-and-ready pubs by the docks. Dressed as I was, I looked like their off-duty butler. They even called me Jeeves.

I learnt mostly on the job. Remembering everyone's names was key, as I was quite clumsy. Even if I spilt a pint, at least I was able to apologise to the person by name, which lessened the blow.

Another trick my Dad employed, which I appropriated, was dealing with a situation where you are 50-50 on someone's name. If you are not sure whether the person in question is Colin or Trevor, look the other way, shout "Colin!" and see if he reacts. People are like dogs, and usually respond to hearing their name in public. If not, try the same with "Trevor!" If you have absolutely no idea, it's probably not the best move to shout random names until you hit the jackpot.

After university, I worked behind the bar at three other pubs. I wouldn't say I was the best barman in the world, but I learnt the basics. By the end, I mastered doing two things at once, while talking to two different people at once. Progress!

My Dos & Don'ts of Pub Customer Service

1   Knowing which customer is next. We Brits might love a queue, but that queue has to be orderly. It is a basic requirement of the bartender to log who has arrived first. A customer who has to say "Excuse me, I'm next" is doing your job for you. There is nothing more infuriating than bar staff with no idea of who is next in line. This sends

panic down the most patient person's spine. I always use to say to someone "You're next", while still serving the previous customer. I found it relaxes a potentially stressful situation. The last thing you want as a bartender is customers bickering, pushing their way in and, worst of all, waving a £20 note at you.

2 Put change in your hand, not in a tray. We have been exchanging money for centuries. Why all of sudden should our change be left on a silver tray. Are these barkeeps expecting a tip, like our American counterparts? We've just queued at the bar, this isn't waiter service. Or are they just too cool to touch a customer?

3 Filling a glass with ice. This is not the cinema. Too much ice is stingy, and robs the customer of their drink. The only time it's acceptable is if the customer actually requests a glass of ice.

4 Have enough bar staff. There is nothing worse than being three deep at the bar, and only one discernible member of staff behind the bar. I appreciate you have to get the balance right, but I think if you don't have enough staff you will lose sales. There are exceptions; for example, when one has to pop down to the cellar to change a barrel.

5 Face the customer, where possible. Pubs should position the till so staff do not have to turn their backs on the customer every time they use it. If fast food restaurants can manage it, so can pubs.

6 Not ordering the right amount of beer and running out. If it is a rare, or seasonal ale, that is understandable. But running out of a session ale or popular lager is careless.

7 Dirty glasses, crockery and utensils. If these are dirty, what is the quality of the food or drink like?

8 Keep the pub tidy. Used pint glasses scattered all over the pub, dirty plates and tossed crisp packets is a no-no, and creates a slovenly atmosphere.

Orwell and Drinking Vessels

In his 'Moon Under Water' essay, Orwell raised the issue of which glass to use and when:

> 'They are particular about their drinking vessels at the Moon Under Water, and never, for example, make the mistake of serving a pint of beer in a handleless glass.'

Personally, I think you give the customer the choice. If I had to state a preference, I like a handleless glass, or sleever, to drink a light or medium beer, and a mug with a handle for a stronger winter ale. These days you can add branded glasses to the mix, which pubs are given free from the supplier. If you are going to use branded glasses, you need to match them with the correct drink. There is nothing worse than an ale served in a Guinness glass or a stout in a Strongbow glass.

Orwell on Addressing Customers

The author also commented on how the barmaids refer to the clientele:

> 'They call everyone 'dear,' irrespective of age or sex.
> ('Dear,' not 'Ducky': pubs where the barmaid calls you 'ducky' always have a disagreeable raffish atmosphere.)'

Similarly, my Dad is disgruntled by bartenders referring to everyone as 'guys', whether you are male or female. It was originally an Americanism, but now seems to be prevalent in young middle class kids on a gap year.

Let's Bounce

Occasionally, inner city pubs have to provide security on the door, especially if that bar is open late. Bouncers are like children; they should be seen and not heard.

The best bit of bouncing I have ever witnessed happened at Jesters' Comedy Pub, Stoke's Croft, Bristol. Some overexuberant nitwit was dancing on a table. He was asked to step down, but refused. Rather than get into an altercation, the bouncer began to dance with him. The doorman took the guy's hand, gave him a twirl, waltzed him off the table and out the door, onto the street. The dancer was none the wiser. That is Strictly Come Bouncing. The doorman was moonlighting as a bouncer; by day, he told me, he was studying politics. We avoided a diplomatic incident that night.

Conclusion

Ultimately, we want to be welcomed into a pub, and served quickly and efficiently. My Mum always says:

> *"If you have a good experience, you tell a couple of people;*
> *if you have a bad experience, you tell everybody!"*

There is a lot of truth in that statement. These days, travel review websites, like Trip Advisor, have put everyone on their guard. Everyone is accountable, although businesses can respond to criticism online.

I can sum up this chapter in three words – common sense required

Lock-Ins

I began this chapter by talking about last, or next orders. It's only appropriate we end with a lock-in.

Licensing laws are a little more relaxed in the sticks, where lock-ins, or drinking after time, are a common occurrence. Once the doors are locked, it's no longer a public bar, but a private party. It's a lovely legal loophole; it's a party, as long as no money changes hands after closing time, although it's perfectly legal to pay for a few bevvies in advance. Drinking is all about thinking.

Everyone loves a lock-in. In most pubs you have to earn the right to be included. The regulars linger over their last pint as the landlord ushers the hoi-polloi out the door. The lock-in is a chance for the landlord and landlady to have a quiet, or sometimes noisy, drink with friends. The shutters are shut, the lights are on low and there is a conspiratorial element to the evening. As my drinking partner, Dominic Frisby, once said, "perfect for a bit of plotting."

During lock-ins, anything seems possible. The lines have been drawn and you're separated from the rest of the world. It's a magical mischievous realm of drunkenness, where the bar is your playground. Why not try that dusty bottle that no one has ever touched? Some of the best stories, daftest ideas, rudest songs, juiciest gossip and mind-boggling myths and facts I've ever heard have all emanated from lock-ins.

LET THE MUSIC PLAY (OR NOT)

19

MUSIC IN PUBS is like Marmite and often divides opinion. Wetherspoon's has a no-music policy and so does my parents' pub. However, an accordionist, harmonica or a ukulele player might emerge from his or her shell, after closing time, for an impromptu singalong.

Scientists have proved that playing music loudly in pubs and bars makes people drink more and faster. The fact that we struggle to hear each other's conversation with loud music playing must also speed up our drinking. Boffins have proved that loud music arouses the brain, making us drink faster. I've never heard this excuse before:

> *"Sorry I drank so much last night, my brain was clearly in a high state of arousal."*

Muzak

Background music or Muzak, the type you hear in a hotel lift or supermarket, is often used to try and cultivate an atmosphere. The pub I worked at while studying at Swansea University had a case of Muzak cassettes which we were advised by the brewery to play. As they are usually poor covers of the classics by session musicians, they sounded fairly humdrum.

One afternoon my friend Toby passed me a tape to play. It was 'The Best of Van Morison'. Van warbled in the background, as folk sipped and slurped their drinks. About an hour later, an elderly gentleman complained of swearing. When I questioned the whereabouts of the bad language, he declared it was seeping from the walls. My first inclination was to calmly dismiss this as a minor eccentricity. But upon investigating his seating area, I too could hear foul language and, more absurdly, cricket commentary. It took me a few seconds to piece together the puzzle. The cassette deck must have possessed auto-reverse. Younger readers may be unaware, but this meant a cassette would automatically play the other side, allowing continuous play. This was cutting edge technology when I was a young gun. Anyhow, at the end of the Van Morrison side the tape reversed and began playing the other side, which was 'Twelfth Man', a cricket commentary show, with a boatload of swearing. I resisted the urge to tell the old gentleman we were cursed with the foul-mouthed ghost of a cricket commentator and flipped back to mo' Van Mo'.

Pipe Down Movement

There is an active campaign against music in pubs, called the Pipe Down Movement.

> *"What do we want?"*
> *"Shhhh."*
> *"When do we want it?"*
> *"I said, shush!"*

George Orwell wrote in his perfect pub essay:

> *'In the Moon Under Water it is always quiet enough to talk. The house possesses neither a radio nor a piano, and even on Christmas Eve and such occasions the singing that happens is of a decorous kind.'*

Live Music

There is a cornucopia of kick-ass pubs specifically dedicated to live music. Growing up in Bristol, the Bristol Bridge, the Blues Bar and the Fleece and Firkin were all gert lush live music pubs. My old flatmate Jukerrr (you cannot call yourself Julian if you work on a building site) was a big fan of a blues guitarist called Eddie Martin, who used to play at all the hard-drinking, easy-listening, pubs in Bristol.

However, we are discussing the accoutrements of the perfect pub, so we will treat music as a delightful bonus, rather than the main focus. In this respect, the occasional singer-songwriter is a welcome asset in certain pubs.

Pub DJ

There is a trend of having a live DJ playing in a pub. Unless it is a pre-club bar, on a weekend, it can sound a trifle naff. My friend, Ali Chambers, is a good DJ and used to have a residency in Las Iguanas, a Mexican bar in Bristol. Unfortunately, as it was a bar, some of the locals mistook him for a mobile disco. I remember the following conversation:

GEEZER: *"'Ere mate, you got any Oasis?"*
DJ ALI: *"Sorry. It's a dedicated drum 'n' bass night."*
GEEZER: *"C'mon! You must have 'Don't Look Back In Anger', it's a bloody classic."*

Karaoke

Karaoke is like discussing politics: fine, but only in the right environment. Karaoke is great fun in the confines of a sound-proof booth or in Japan, but a living hell in an open-plan pub. Don't get me wrong, I'm not a purist; my singing voice is so bad I have to mime at football matches. When it comes to singing, I always 'Walk Alone'.

In my old West Country local, The Swan, in Tockington, they used to hold karaoke on Boxing Day night, and one of the kitchen porters used to dance to it. It reminded me of the great northern comedian and poet Hovis Presley, now sadly deceased, who had a poem called 'The Girl Who Danced to Announcements,' about how she would boogie while the DJ inquired whose Ford Sierra was blocking the fire exit.

Jukeboxes

An old jukebox can be a delightful perk in a pub, providing the 'juke' on offer is from fairly good bands. The jukebox is the iPod shuffle for the older generation.

The best story I have heard on the subject is from the New York comedian John Mulaney, who tells a hilarious tale about loading a jukebox with coins, and putting Tom Jones' 'What's New Pussycat' on continuous play. Do look it up online; it is five minutes of gut-laughing hilarity.

Rock 'n' Roll Pubs

There are also pubs that are heavily associated with music. For example, The Hawley Arms in Camden was home to such luminaries as Amy Winehouse, Razorlight and Mark Ronson. Amy was even known to step behind the bar and help out occasionally.

Garlic and Shots on Frith Street in Soho is a rock 'n' roller's destination of choice and does exactly what it says on the tin. They specialise in garlic and serve 101 different flavoured vodka shots. The heavy metal music is loud too, so you can drink fast, and leave with garlic breath and a minor ear ache.

Growing up in Bristol, the musician's' hang out was The Bell on Jamaica Street. The Stoke's Croft area is awash with hipsters these days, but in my day this was a grimy enclave. It was the regular watering hole for Massive Attack and you'd regularly see 3D, Daddy G and their entourage, kicking back there. No one bothered them, apart from a few girls, which they never seemed to mind.

One of my favourite late night pubs is The Washington Arms, in Sheffield, known locally as The Washy. The Last Laugh comedy club promoter, Jules, loves to take acts here after shows and it is a brilliant late-night haunt. The pub attracts musicians and counts Pulp among its regulars. Whenever I go there I always fall into conversation with Pulp's old tour manager, who regales me of stories of 'Bloody 'Awley' and 'Tha' nitwit Jarv'. He is like an old schoolmaster admonishing his famous pupils; no wonder they are so down to earth as a band. I performed my Perfect Pub show here as a double-header with Paul Sinha from ITV's *The Chase*. We had a lock-in and had full use of the jukebox, which Paul DJ'd, conjuring up such old classics as Nik Kershaw's 'Wouldn't It Be Good'. It certainly was.

Whether you are for or against music in pubs, never fear, in future we will probably all be condemned to wearing headphones regardless. These headphones will be noise cancelling, unless you want a thick ear from the Pipe Down movement.

With my Dad and sister, Talia, outside the Bristol Hippodrome Stage Door.

PUB GAMES AND ENTERTAINMENT

20

FROM FLYING DARTS TO DRUNKEN HECKLES

NOW THAT some pubs are becoming our communal front rooms and playrooms again, as mentioned in the opening chapter, it is only natural we let the games begin.

Quiz Nights

Quiz nights are very popular, and a fine way of drumming up trade on an otherwise quiet night.

According to *Guinness World Records*, the first ever British quiz is reported to have taken place at York Working Men's Club in September 1946 – which is a good question in itself. When quizzes started in pubs is uncertain, but it is suggested they were inspired by quiz shows on TV and radio.

Aside from winning, arguably the most important part of any quiz night is thinking up a devilishly witty and fiendishly funny team name. I think BBC2's *University Challenge* would be infinitely more entertaining if they were allowed to coin their own team names.

Why is it, even though the pun has mostly retired from humour, that it excels in tabloid headlines and quiz team names? There are certain classic team names which crop up regularly: Quiz Akabusi, Quiz-lamic Fundamentalists, Quiz Quiz-stoffersen, to name a few.

There are three elements to a good pub quiz: the host, the prize and the difficulty of questions. The host doesn't have to be funny, just interesting. There are a few wacky hosts who have a whiff of commercial radio DJ about them, and the result is cringeworthy. My friend Luke, who hosts a few quiz nights near me, is quietly cheeky, but never patronising. I also like an ageing eccentric. There was a portly chap who used to host a weekly quiz at The Bailey, in Highbury, who called himself The Fat Controller. He had a lovely charm, in the manner of Richard Griffiths. Our gang liked him so much we followed him to his other quiz in The Florence, on Upper Street.

The prize needs to be reasonably good; a food and drinks tab for the place you're quizzing in is perfect. I first met Luke at the Soho House Quiz. While the socialites were socialising and trading bon mots, my friends and I were focusing. We needed to win, as we didn't have the coffers to eat or drink there otherwise. We were literally quizzing for our supper, and when we won, boy did victory taste good.

I believe the perfect quiz question requires an answer that is on the tip of your tongue, an answer you need to stretch for. I once attended a film quiz at the Clapham Picturehouse, which was impossible. The host would choose a genre (you see, 'genre'; already we're using pretentious language). He would mention everything you might know about the subject in the preamble to the question and then ask some left-field question. It was no fun whatsoever. I almost made a point by leaving with my pint unfinished. But that is just cutting off your pint to spite your face.

Pool

My game of choice is pool. The most important part of pub pool is having enough space to stretch your cue and play your shot. There is nothing more hampering than having to hug a wall and point your cue ceilingwards, in a vague attempt to scuff the ball instead of the wall. Even worse are those short half-cues some places provide. I am not a hobbit or a half-ling, just a guy looking for some smooth cue action. I would love to play pool with members of the Swiss army. I am sure their cues would be multipurpose, extendable, with separate sockets for a rest, chalk and a corkscrew.

According to Arthur Taylor, in his intriguing book, *Played in the Pub: The Pub Games of Britain*:

> *'No fewer than 85 different games have borne the name "pool" since it was first mentioned in an 1819 edition of* Hoyle's Games.'

He goes on to explain that the word pool is derived from the French word *poule*, normally chicken but here meaning kitty or stake. The origin lies in gambling. So if you do hustle at pool, you are merely playing the game in the way in which it was intended.

My favourite pub to play pool in used to be The Hillgrove, in Stoke's Croft, Bristol. I used to go there on Friday nights, with my bookish comrades from Waterstones. The pool table was set in a raised area, with stools around for a grandstand view. It was the classic 'Winner Stays On', but unfortunately I was rarely away from my mates for long. I seemed to be playing my own game of 'Loser Stays Clear'. One time I went on a small winning streak and swaggered back to our table, only to find my lot thought I'd been loitering in the loo.

The best player I have ever played against is the comedian Sean Meo. He was a semi-pro snooker player, before becoming a first class joke-slinger. Even his comedy routines are short jokes, which he builds into a break. I will never forget the last game we had: he broke, turned away and joked with a friend. Meanwhile, I plopped all my balls in the pockets, leaving only the black. I didn't cheat, I just feel 'plopping' accurately describes my style of gently rolling them into the pocket, rather than rocketing them home, in the manner of 'Fast Eddie' Felsom or Vince from *The Colour of Money*. Anyhow, Sean looked round to see me miss or miss-plop the black. He calmly collected himself, and thwacked, whacked, whizzed, top-spinned, back-spinned, and humdingered his way to an empty table. On potting the black thunderously in the corner pocket, he casually turned his gaze upon me, and deadpanned, "You know what your problem is? You missed one!"

On his last visit to the UK, I asked my new brother-in-law, M-H, what he wished for in his perfect pub. He said, "I never go to a pub that hasn't got a pool table!"

I am pleased to discover that M-H is a pool fanatic, and even competes in professional competitions. Leo and I recently watched him play in the final of a tournament online. He lives in Wisconsin, in the United States, and his job is making and restoring pool tables. I am sure he would be happy to fashion a custom-made table for our perfect pub.

I took M-H to Skehans, a local Peckham pub with a pool table. It was a Saturday lunchtime, and M-H caused a stir in the pub, by bringing his own cue. He narrowly beat me on the black on our first game, but once he ascertained I wasn't dreadful, he upped his game slightly, and gave me a sound thrashing. In between games, I asked him his thoughts on bar pool:

M-H Pool Interview

M-H: *"I think it's interesting, the difference between English and American pool. I like English balls better, because all your balls are the same colour, so it's much easier to read the table. On an American table, you have solids and stripes, but every single ball is a different colour."*

ME: *"You brought your own cue. What makes it worth bringing on an international flight, with a limited luggage allowance?"*

M-H: *"Ha! I love this cue. I've always wanted a three-piece cue, where all three sections are the same length. Each section is short, so you can actually put this cue in your pocket. Walk into a bar, stick it under your shirt..."*

ME: *"It's like a sniper's rifle."*

M-H: *"Yeah, it is. In America, they call them Sneaky Petes. They look like bar cues, but the joints are hidden, so when you put it together it looks like a one-piece bar cue, and so when you're hustling, people don't think you're using your own cue. You have a nice cue, with a good finish and a good tip, and it's the same cue you always use, so you have consistency."*

ME: *"That is sneaky. Also, if you have a tight shot in the corner, and you're not hustling, you can remove a section."*

Finally, as a guy blessed with a lazy eye I often like to look away from the cue ball, pretending I can still see it. I can't of course, but I have perfected the art of potting balls without looking. The problem is, people are more impressed if I say I am using my wonky eye, rather than employing actual skill. I imagine magicians would agree with this sentiment. Explaining how a trick works can ruin the mystique and the awe the magic trick should inspire.

Billiards

Some ye olde pubs have a billiards table. This is not to be confused with bar billiards, which is a different game entirely, involving pin skittles and nine holes on the table, rather than in the corner. Bar billiards is appropriately named, as I'm generally good at pub sports, barring billiards. I never acquired the knack, surprisingly really, as part of the point of billiards is to pot the white or cue ball. To watch me play snooker or pool, you would think I'd be an absolute natural. I'm always potting the white.

Darts

Another old-fashioned game that has lasted the distance is darts. Unfortunately, my Dad has recently retired his pub board. Back in the 1980s it hung proudly at one end of the public bar. George Orwell would approve. In the 'The Moon Under Water' he wrote:

> *'Games are only played in the public, so that in the other bars you can walk about without constantly ducking to avoid flying darts.'*

As a kid, I loved darts. We played 'Around the Clock', 'Killer' and my favourite, 'Nearest the Board'. The latter was invented by Jonny Dyke, my aforementioned Irish companion, and I. The rules were simple: you had three darts to hit the target; if you hit the board, you took a step back on your next go. By the end of the game, we were standing at the other end of the bar and hurling darts like Fatima Whitbread's javelins. We often had to stand on a bar stool to help us pick the stray ones out of the ceiling. By the end of the school holidays that ceiling looked like a pin cushion, whereas the dart board was still disappointingly pristine.

The last time I played darts was in the Three Compasses, in Dalston, a few years ago. Also, it was in a hipster pub, so it probably doesn't count! You don't see so many dartboards these days. Maybe because, like snooker and pool, they are deemed to take up too much valuable floor space.

Table Football

The other game I loved as a kid, and still enjoy playing in a pub today, has a variety of names. You may call it table football, babyfoot, or foosball, depending on whether you're English, French or American. Joey and Chandler were constantly having bets on the outcome of their foosball matches, in the hit sitcom *Friends*. Incidentally, the American term foosball is used most widely and derives from the German word, fussball. The latter sounds like it was named by someone who did not approve of the game.

According to Arthur Taylor, in his book mentioned earlier, the first foosball table was made by the French firm, Breve Simon, in 1903. No wonder the French are so good at it. It is rumoured that Eric Cantona is an enthusiast. My French friend, Laurent Pujos, employs incredible control and is able to dribble with the ball. I just dribble. I am more a traditional 'hit and hope' kind of guy. No spinning though; that's cheating.

I like playing with four players best, and usually elect to play goalie and defence, the advantage being that it is often easier to score with your defenders, who seem to be able to belt it like Beckham or Bale.

Morecambe and Wise performed an amusing sketch where they pretended to be the players on a table football pitch. They discuss matters while jockeying from left to right, performing high kicks, and doing somersaults. Look it up online. It's hilarious.

Board Games

Board games have had a resurgence in pubs. You can often spot a few folk playing Battleships or Connect 4 on a Sunday afternoon. My personal favourite is a role-playing card game called Citadels. The only game I personally object to is Jenga, in particular giant Jenga, as it makes such an almighty clatter every five or 10 minutes, followed by a scream, whoop and a cheer. In the old days, we relied upon a clumsy waiter or waitress to create such a disturbance.

Skittles and Pétanque

'Life isn't all beer and skittles,' was the famous phrase from *Tom Brown's School Days* by Thomas Hughes. A game of skittles sounds old fashioned now, but the quote was from a book written in 1857. The important point is that skittles was a pub game and therefore went in hand in hand with drinking a beer. There is still a league where I grew up in the West Country.

My Dad's pub favours pétanque, which is a form of boules. The home team is even called The Petanchors. A few of the regulars used to play in the gravelly car park over the road. The game really took off in 1982, when they challenged a rival pub to a match. It proved so popular, my Dad converted a small orchard out the back into a proper pétanque terrain. It might sounds excessive, but there was method in my Dad's madness; pétanque players get thirsty and are happy to play on quiet nights of the week. Even on a hot summer's night they are drinking out the back, leaving plenty of room for others in the bar.

Stand-Up Comedy Nights

Call me biased for throwing this last suggestion in the mix, but a quality well-run comedy night is always good-value entertainment. I purposely preface this with 'well-run', as there is nothing more cringeworthy than a poorly organised comedy show. The late '90s and early Noughties were boom time for the comedy industry and big clubs ruled the roost. Since the recession live comedy has downscaled, but this is still great news for pubs.

You can now find live comedy in, above, below and behind pubs. As a touring comedian, I am therefore lucky enough to call pubs my workplace, and I can even drink on the job.

Through gigging I have discovered all manner of hidden gems. The Bedford in Balham, South London, is a barnstormingly good pub. It's rare that a pub this size has a core of regular drinkers. My friend Andrew Bird used to work behind the bar here, before becoming a comedian. They have a Shakespearian Globe-style theatre at the back which hosts the famous Banana Cabaret, one of the oldest and best comedy rooms, which has been running for 30 years. They also provide live music and regular dance classes. It really is a one-stop shop for a myriad of entertainment.

Crouch End hosts the equally long-serving Downstairs at the Kings Head. This is a delightful well-heeled pub, at the foot of Crouch End Hill. Upstairs they serve craft ales, artisan lagers and boast a good food menu while, in the basement, comedy ensues. It is the perfect comedy room too, low ceiling, soft lighting and good acoustics.

In central London I recommend The Phoenix on Cavendish Square, which is only a few minutes' walk from Oxford Circus tube. On Monday nights they host a new material night called Old Rope. It plays host to well-known and sometimes famous comedians trialling jokes before committing them to the goggle box. The bar upstairs has a good selection of ales, and its proximity to Oxford Street makes it the perfect bolthole to recover from a bout of Christmas shopping.

I have to give a special mention to John Hatch. Following the sale of Young's Ram Brewery in Wandsworth in 2006, John kept a promise to John Young to keep brewing on the site. With the help of comedian, Al Cowlie, John runs a comedy night to raise funds for his brewing. There is no licence for beer sales, so unfortunately it is a free bar. You just have to buy a ticket to the comedy. Here is a fantastic example of stand-up comedy helping the brewing community. I have performed there more than most and his Pheonix (4.3% ABV), an English-style pale, is an absolute doozy. According to John:

> "It is brewed using Maris Otter malted barley and Golding hops. It is not overly bitter, or hoppy, and has characteristics of dried fruit and marmalade."

If you're ever in Bristol, The Hen & Chickens in Bedminster plays host to The Comedy Box at the weekend. It is where I performed my first-ever gigs. The pub was originally a rough and ready den of iniquity and popular with diehard Bristol City fans, so comedians risked dying both in the bar as well as on stage, but it has now morphed into a gastro-pub, as the area has gentrified. You can often catch some fairly big names on tour here.

The Barrack Inn, Sheffield, is a fabulous family-run pub with a plethora of Yorkshire ales and humour to match. The front bar is reminiscent of a parlour room and you feel immediately at home. Their comedy night runs on a Sunday.

I have already mentioned The Grainstore in Oakham, but all credit to the staff for turning the main bar into a decent comedy venue that attracts punters from miles around. Gloucester Brewery also run a fantastic comedy room in the brewery tap, on the Gloucester Quay. In place of a backdrop are shelves and shelves of bottled craft ales.

My Worst Night as a Stand-Up

I ought to balance matters by mentioning my least-favourite comedy night, held in a pub. This particular pub, in Maidstone, is thankfully under wonderful new management, still runs comedy, and is prospering nicely. The original comedy night ran for 15 or so years, and prided itself on being a belligerent heckle fest. Most comedians have a death story from this dank corner of Kent. If Kent is the garden of England, parts of Maidstone must rank as the compost heap.

The format of the evening was thus: every Thursday a hapless comedian pitched up, the plug of the fruit machine was yanked out, the landlord yelled at the masses to stop talking and listen to a comedian, who took his or her place on the stage – sorry a box in the corner. It was the comedian's job to grab the microphone provided, and attempt to entertain the rabble for 40 minutes, with no warm up act.

Once in a while, a fellow comic will enquire whether the Maidstone story they have heard about me is true.

"Yes. Absolutely." I reply. This is the story they are referring to. In 2004 I was booked in to do the gig by my former agent Lisa White, who still regards the following as the funniest thing attributed to me. Before I headed out that night, my former flatmate, Dominic Frisby, confided in me that while onstage at this gig he bent over and some geezer pulled down his trousers and slapped his bum. It is not only your dignity that gets stripped here.

The night in question, I entered the pub to be greeted by a barrage of testosterone, stale cigarette fumes and Lynx deodorant. A crowd of close-shaved heads in Burberry shirts and white Reebok Classic loitered at the bar, guzzling strong continental lager. At the time I looked rather studenty, with a plaid shirt and an unruly mop of long curly hair. As I queued at the bar, I overheard two knuckleheads joshing:

"Comedian arrived yet?"
"Hope not. They're usually shit."

With that, all the confidence drained from my young face. I cannot explain the rationale for what I did next, maybe it was because I was run down, or because of the stories I had heard previously, but I exited the pub, clambered back into my car and called the pub, asking to speak to the landlord. I informed him my car had broken down and I couldn't make the gig. Barely a minute into the conversation and there was a tap on the driver's side window and behold, there was the landlord, with a cordless phone and a huge grin.

LANDLORD: *"Shall we keep talking or do you want to open the window?"*
ME: *"I'm so sorry."*
LANDLORD: *"Ha ha! I saw you walk in mate, turnaround and walk out. Ha ha! I clocked you straightaway. You look different to my lot. Don't worry, you're not the first to bottle it.*

I've had some of the best acts in the country get out of my gig.
Cognito didn't fancy it, Sadowitz neither. I fink Russell Brand
was up for it, but 'e might 'ave been on 'eroin at the time.
Now I'll grab you a pint and we'll kick off in 20 minutes."

Rather than being surprised, the landlord seemed to be almost proud of the menacing reputation his gig held. I vaguely remember the show going OK, but the pre-show was certainly charred into my memory. I returned to the scene of the crime 12 years later, now under new management, and received a warm welcome on a balmy summer's evening. The pub now garners a lovely clientele and is more lauded than *Loaded* magazine. The food is delicious and the bar showcases numerous ales from local breweries. The comedy continues every Thursday and there are now two acts rather than one. Progress.

It seems if we are to incorporate a comedy night, pool, and table football, we will need a separate function room. This also means a quiz night could be run in there too, meaning non-quizzers won't have their conversations interrupted by a quizmaster bellowing out questions.

TV, WI-FI, PHONES AND MOANS

21

Television Always Splits the Crowd

Those in favour will always put forward an argument for live sport. To be fair, there is something special about watching your team play, with a pub atmosphere. I am an ardent Aston Villa fan, so any atmosphere is welcome when cheering on my team – although, perhaps, cheering up is more appropriate.

I remember watching Villa take on Liverpool in a packed Scouse pub next to The Cavern. The pub was called Flanagan's Apple and it is famous for being the first Irish-theme pub in the UK, but that day the theme was Liverpool FC. It was like watching your team in the away end, or operating undercover. Everything was "Boss la", which means "Rather good young man", until my team inadvertently scored. My spine jolted, my body twitched, but my mouth held still, like a true ventriloquist. I had to duck into the gents for a silent whoop. "Gabby! You beauty." The scorer was Villa's former cult hero Gabby Agbonlahor. If I ever meet him, I would love to tell him I celebrated his goal in a Liverpudlian lavatory.

The World Cup is a perfect time to watch football in the pub, unless of course there is a suspicious amount of England flags, then perhaps it's to be avoided.

Sky Sports

When you watch Sky Sports in a pub, you might spot a little pint glass in the bottom right-hand corner of the screen. The more eagle-eyed among you may have even spied the level of the pint glass changing. The reason is money. A pub subscription to Sky Sports is more expensive than a home subscription, so the pint glass confirms that your pub has paid its sub, and is not just broadcasting from a home account. It might seem rather petty, but it is worth millions of pounds. The reason the level of the pint glass varies is because some bright sparks put a small sticker on the screen, to make it look like they'd paid. The level change guards against this and makes it easier for the inspectors to know what to look for. What a petty job, like a TV licensing detector van, with a badge.

The Three Sisters pub I performed at in Edinburgh, in 2015, was renowned for its huge outdoor TV screen. Along with its cobbled courtyard, the TV screen draws the crowds on weekends. It was always full when a big game was on, whether it was football or rugby. Perhaps an outdoor screen is worth considering for our perfect pub. We could create our own Henman Hill or Murray Mound from which to watch.

While at Swansea university, I was amazed at the effect rugby had on the town. When Wales played international rugby, every bar was teeming with supporters. It's not often you hear hymns being sung in a pub, but 'Bread Of Heaven' reverberates right around the valleys on match days. Unlike, football fans, they can actually sing. It is like a drunken choir.

Watching sport on a pub TV also seems to be a good way of distracting a stag do or hen party, until the real drinking starts.

The Perfect Spot to Watch Sport

Some sports fans do take it a step too far. Oli Gross reported in *The Morning Advertiser* (pub trade press), in June 2016, that a maths expert, called Hongshueng Dai, working in conjunction with PC World, devised a mathematical formula to predict the perfect spot to watch football in a pub. Their findings state:

> *'Viewers should sit 1.6 times the screen size away from the TV. By this calculation fans should sit 70.4 inches away from a 44-inch screen for the optimum view.'*

PC World went on to suggest that this formula should be used to reward loyal customers with the best seat and naughtier members with the worst. Although it doesn't take a scientist or mathematician to work out whether you can see the screen or are a little too close to the toilets for comfort.

The article expands its theory:

> *'It's not just about the distance from the TV, as the formula suggests sport is (best) viewed from a 30 degree angle from the centre of the TV.'*

Personally, this is the sort of psychobabble I thrive upon. I love the idea of a football fan prizing open his trigonometry set and fumbling with his protractor, to determine the best position to whoop and holler for his team. Perhaps even measuring out the distance from the TV with a tape measure.

Objecting to Televisions in Pubs

Those who object to TV often say it's a barrier to good conversation. George Orwell, in his perfect pub essay, required:

> *'A pub quiet enough to talk, possessing neither TV or radio.'*

Wetherspoon's follows this dictum to the letter. To be fair, it's sometimes hard to concentrate when you are distracted by something colourful and shiny moving across a hypnotic screen. When I'm in a pub with a television, I have to sit with the TV behind me, as I don't trust myself not to watch. Silly really, as I have a lazy eye and could easily view both. Having said that, I don't think my brain is up to the multi-tasking involved.

My Dad always felt the pub was a way of escaping the hypnotic eye of the gogglebox. A few years ago, The Anchor's trade slowed down a little on Saturday nights. He realised a few of the regulars were staying in to watch *Strictly Come Dancing*. To counteract this, on Saturday nights The Anchor offers a dish of the day, at a reduced price. The name of this promo: Strictly Come Dining. It has been a great success. The pub is packed again and some people are happy to get their *Strictly* fix on BBC iPlayer later.

A few weeks into writing this book, I tried writing in a pub. It seemed like the perfect plan, to write about pubs, in a pub. Maybe it helps to be at one with your subject, like Hunter S. Thompson, Jack Kerouac, Bruce Robinson or, indeed, George Orwell. I settled at a table with a pint of Tribute, and began writing in my notebook. However, I only averaged a pint a paragraph, not as prolific as I intended writing-wise, and far too much, beer-wise. To be fair, it wasn't all my fault. I was only a few sentences in, when a projector screen was unfurled, to show the football.

Arsenal were playing Bayern Munich in the Champions League. A lovely group of German lads sat down next to me and watched the football, without a pint between them. One thing I do know, is that German people love a pint as much as we Brits do. Realising the problem, I advised them to order at the bar; no table service here. I also informed them if they are not sure what to drink, they can try before they buy. They thought I was joking. After reassuring them, they traded up from vier Becks Vier to four foaming pints of Doom Bar. There were other ales on offer, but I thought recommending a pint of Spitfire to a table of Germans might seem a trifle insensitive.

I recently watched a football match at The Compton Arms, Islington, one of Orwell's favourite watering holes. I was there with a talented actor friend and pub connoisseur, David Ahmad. He stated it was the classiest pub in North London to show Sky Sports! I wonder what Orwell would think. I am fairly certain he would have a strong take on Mr Murdoch and his global empire.

Wi-Fi

There was a famous punk song by Splodgenessabounds, a one-hit wonder from Peckham, called 'Two pints of lager and a packet of crisps please'; nowadays that would be 'Two craft ales, wasabi nuts and the Wi-Fi code please.'

I think Wi-Fi should be free everywhere. Are you listening hotels? So extending free Wi-Fi to pubs is fine by me. The only time I object is when a sign declaring 'Free Wi-Fi' seems to be the main selling point of the pub. Besides, having readily available Wi-Fi enables punters to 'check in' on Facebook. My friend Mark Dodds, who is a pioneer of the Peoples Pub Partnership, which is responsible for saving, improving and reinvigorating pubs, checks in to every pub he visits, as a matter of course.

Businesses are very keen on us checking in and tagging our visits to their establishments as part of the social media phenomenon. Do you know who else checks in to places to let others know they've been there? Dogs. They tag their movements with wee, wherever they go.

Having Wi-Fi used to give pubs an edge on their competitors, but now it is expected. I think it is not enough to have Wi-Fi, it needs to work consistently throughout the pub and not just in one corner. We don't want people wandering willy-nilly trying to find the place with the optimum reception. We have enough trigonometry happening with the nerd trying to find the best spot to watch TV.

Plug sockets aplenty are a must, especially with smartphone batteries running low at a frustrating rate. There is a generation of us who on entering a pub will immediately scan for free plug sockets.

Whether we like it or not, smartphones are here to stay. The Ace Hotel, in Shoreditch, East London, has small docking stations on its tables, from which you can recharge your phone or laptop. We could have a few of these, installed or integrated subtly, into the furniture.

A few years ago when my flat Wi-Fi was down I queued outside a pub at opening time along with a few others in order to use the facilities. What better hot desk is there than a perch in your favourite pub?

Mobile Phones

Some folk object to mobiles in the pub, preferring to see it as an oasis of calm of tranquillity. My Dad claimed that virtually no one ever used a mobile in his pub. It was not until he eventually got one himself that he realised it was because the pub was situated in a dip at the foot of a hill and had no phone signal.

The first mobile phone ever used in my Dad's pub was attributed to a guy called Michael Good. He claimed to be in the music industry, touring with the Rolling Stones and a regular on the festival circuit including Glastonbury. He was. He provided all the portaloos. He pitched up at The Anchor one lunchtime, with the first mobile I ever saw. Although I say mobile, it was almost immobile, it was so heavy. Remember the Nokia brick? Well this was the breeze block. He used to heave it onto the bar for all to see. But no one ever called.

One day, my Dad's bar manager, Peter Riley, sourced the number and rang it, from the out the back. There was a deafening roar; the old army colonel shouted "Air raid!"; my Mum thought it was the fire alarm. Eventually, everyone clocked the phone shuddering and shaking like an old washing machine on spin cycle. Michael grappled with it, winched it to his ear and yelled "Good here!" for all to hear. The voice on the other end was heard to say: "Michael, your scampi is ready." None of the villagers rushed to buy a phone after that.

I read in the trade press that a new cocktail bar, called The Gin Tub, in East Sussex, has blocked mobile phone signals, in a bid to encourage its customers to quit gawping at their screens and talk to each other directly instead. The owner, Steve Tyler, said he wanted to force "people to interact in the real world" and claims social media is killing pubs. He has a Batman-style electronic shield built into the walls and ceiling to stop the signals penetrating the building. What tickled me was he has also inputted old style phones, for drinkers to order drinks or chat to other tables. It would have cheaper and easier to buy a bar in a dip, like my Dad inadvertently did.

PUB DOGS AND OTHER ANIMALS

22

I F YOU LOOK carefully under the seats in my Dad's pub, you can often spy pairs of glowing eyes. There is nothing quite like a well-trained pub dog, undetected like a sniper, until a food scrap is carelessly dropped. Then with the speed of a starving snake or Hungry Hippo, the treat is sniffed, snaffled and scoffed. The eyes return to the lookout position, as if nothing ever happened.

Types of Pub Dog

A pub dog is a welcoming sight, a sign of homeliness. There are three types of pub dog. The first is the resident pub dog, owned by the landlords. He or she is known to all, lolling by the fireside like royalty, awaiting strokes and treats, rising only to prowl the nooks and crannies of the bar for titbits.

Next are the dog regulars who are acknowledged along with their owners:

"Evening Paul. Evening Poppy."
"Evening all."
"Woof-woof!"

These dogs often have their own spot, just like their owners. Some arrive post-dog walk; for others, unfortunately, the trip to the pub is their walk.

The third type, are the occasional visitors. These dogs are more likely to be kept on a lead, rather than roaming the premises.

Most of the resident pub dogs I have met tend to be older, probably because a puppy, however cute, isn't as cute when cocking its leg on your new suede shoes, so tends to be kept upstairs. In dog years, they reach the drinking age of 18 at two and a half. I like to think, maybe that's part of it.

I love a good pub dog. In fact, I would go so far as to say, I would like to be reincarnated as a resident pub dog. I like plenty of attention, cuddles and eating peanuts off the floor. I do these things anyway; at least now I'd have a good excuse. The only task I'd struggle with is standing on my hind legs to play snooker, while posing for an artist's portrait.

Taking Your Dog to the Pub

I used to look after my friend Dom's dog, a delightful poodle called Frodo. Great name to shout outside a branch of Forbidden Planet; it really excites the nerds. Whenever I walked into our local the bar staff would make a fuss, produce a dog bowl and chat to me. Interestingly, when I went in without Frodo, the bar staff didn't even recognise me. To them, I must have been the cute dog's ugly mate.

Leo runs a doggie daycare, so we often have dogs boarding. On a weekend that may involve calling in to a pub, after a long walk, or walkies.

Walkies is a saccharine word, but certainly gets the doggies revved up for action. Could the act of barking on a walk be called Walkie Talkies?

We live in a city, so before setting out on a trip to a pub, we have to check if it is dog-friendly. Leo and I recently had a week's holiday in Craft Hole, in south-east Cornwall. Nearly everyone seemed to have a dog, and all the pubs we visited nearby were dog-friendly.

In the old days I imagine most pubs would allow dogs, but now with food served in nearly all pubs, some decree it to be unhygienic. They'll be banning pigs next, despite the fact everyone knows they are the cleanest of animals.

When I was looking after Frodo (mentioned above), my friend Dom said:

"When a pub says 'No Dogs', they don't mean Frodo."

Frodo is a cute, well-behaved poodle so can squeeze into the corner of a pub without causing a commotion, or anyone noticing. As the saying goes, 'It is easier to seek forgiveness, than get permission.'

Leo and I recently enjoyed some Thai food at a local pub. Dogs were supposedly not welcome, but the dog we had with us that day was exceedingly cute. He is a tiny Teacup Maltese Terrier: only a half pint, snow white, with a beautifully cute face. He has the best name for a South London dog: Boss. He is still

Boss in the pub

intact, i.e. has balls so, despite his size, he thinks he really is The Boss. Given half the chance, he would hump any dog that moved. Leo approached the bar, with Boss settled into a doggie carrier bag. His head was poking from the top, all angelic and adorable. It was decreed he would be fine in the garden. Boss one, pub nil.

To raise money for a dog charity, I hosted a comedy night in my local pub, the aforementioned Ivy House, in Nunhead. We needed somewhere super dog-friendly, where audience members could bring their dogs, if they wished. We had 85 humans attend and 15 dogs!

All the dogs were on their best behaviour and the only time they barked was when I prompted a response. I spied one of our dogs we look after, a cute black spaniel called Rufus. He looked confused and I thought that he didn't recognise me out of context. Leo pointed out afterwards that he could only hear my voice blasting from the speakers, so ran towards them instead of me. This was a perfectly logical response. When he did spot me, I called him on stage and he leapt into my arms. The only dog to heckle me was Frodo, but to be fair I was talking about him at the time. "That's me he's talking about everyone," he must have yapped.

The headline act was a talented ventriloquist, called Paul Zerdin. We were worried his puppets might excite the dogs, but fortunately they remained calm. No cat puppets thankfully. It was a fantastic night. We not only raised £840 for a dog charity, but also proved how well behaved our pub pooches can be. The trick is your dog needs practice and regular trips to the pub!

According to an article in *The Morning Advertiser* on 30th August 2017 entitled 'Pubs Are a Dog Owner's Best Friend', Fred A'Court writes:

'Walks, it seems, means more than just taking the pooch for a stroll. Almost all dog owners (95%) pay a visit to their local pub and more than a quarter (26%) drop in more than once a week, according to the latest research.'

It just goes to show that dog-friendly pubs are big business. There is now even an award for the most dog-friendly pub. The initiative was launched in 2017 and the first winner was the Hand in Hand, Wimbledon. Let's hope the YouTube sensation Fenton is a regular there. Although he initially rose to fame chasing deer, while his owner in turn chased him despairingly, through Richmond Park, he was also spotted, or heard, frolicking on Wimbledon Common. Maybe the temptation of deer was too much for him.

To this end there is a plethora of websites and apps dedicated to researching the best pubs for your pooch. The one I use is: www.doggiepubs.org.uk

It has a cute subtitle: 'Find out where you and your best friend are welcome.'

This reference site has over 500 recommendations, and they are genuine recommendations; pubs do not pay to be included. The website is user-friendly; just pop in your postcode and it will generate all the dog-friendly pubs in your neighbourhood. There are also little icons describing whether there is food, how adventurous that food is, and whether you and your doggie could stay over. Let's face it, a trip to the pub will be a lot easier when your dog is able to drive you home. Futuristic inventions aside, it still assumes you have a teetotal dog.

In Newcastle and Australia they've released Dog Beer – a beer for dogs. It's non-alcoholic, non-fizzy and tastes of beef. Correct me if I'm wrong, but that's Bovril. Besides, it's not really aimed at dogs, it's for people who fancy having a beer with their dog.

Legislation on Dogs in Pubs

While researching dog-friendly pubs, I stumbled across an edict by The Food Standards Agency, published in 2014, stating:

> 'Food businesses are responsible to ensure their own food safety management procedures identify and control risks to food hygiene such as having adequate procedures in place to prevent domestic animals from having access to places where food is prepared, handled and/or stored.'

I was completely unaware of this ruling. So dogs ARE legally allowed in pubs, as long as they do not interfere with food preparation or food storage. This means the decision to allow dogs in pubs rests solely on the landlords, and whether they feel their kitchen and storage areas are suitably protected against domestic animals. So the fact that Boss, the dog mentioned in the previous story, was so small, meant the bar manager thought he was unthreatening enough to sit in the garden. Good job Leo didn't refer to him by name.

I saw a pub sign which tickled me recently. It said:

> "Dogs welcome but please keep your child on a leash."

Dogs don't ask for much. All they require is a bowl of water, especially in hot weather. A nice touch is a treat jar on the bar, which I've seen in the Hare and Billet on Blackheath.

Doctor Who and K9

After a heavy bit of legislation, let's lighten the mood with a little Hollywood tittle-tattle.

There's a delightfully modest scriptwriter who drinks in my parents' public bar. His name is Bob Baker. He received an Oscar for his work alongside Nick Park in scripting *The Wrong Trousers*. He was allegedly mid-pint when he dreamt up the name Shaun the Sheep.

Bob began his scriptwriting career alongside Dave Martin.

Their big break was writing the Tom Baker years of *Doctor Who*. Where was their think tank of ideas? Why, none other than the public bar of The Anchor. Fuelled on rough cider, Bob had a lightbulb moment, and envisioned Doctor Who having a robot dog called K9. It was a big hit and he still owns the rights to the name.

A few years ago, Steven Spielberg was toying with the idea of a spin-off movie centring around K9. He flew into Bristol on a private jet and was chauffeur-driven down muddy back lanes to The Anchor. No one recognised Bob's new companion, although Spielberg was sporting a flat hat and a wax jacket, so the locals just presumed he was a visiting pig farmer or gamekeeper.

Pub Cats

My audiences have chosen a pub dog as a requirement for the perfect pub in about one in three shows, making it pretty popular. Only one person chose a pub cat, which I'm surprised at. One of our cats, Pickle, is currently hovering over the keyboard as I write. I imagine he is partially attracted to the screen glow and also wondering what could possibly hold my interest more than stroking him. I'll let him put his case forward...

"Fahd vhcdvhbnb jhfjhhllm"

What that means we'll never know. But he is purring so I think it's positive. Feel free to show it to your cat on a kindle, perhaps pump up the brightness, and see what they think.

Incidentally, our kitten Pickle is named after a night drinking Pickle Backs (a shot of whisky mixed with pickle juice), with my Swansea Uni mates, Hippy Jim, Panky and Stu.

The Bag o' Nails pub in Bristol prides itself on being sprawled with cats. The landlord, Luke Daniels, told *The Evening Post*:

"We have 15 cats in the pub. We once had 24, but that was too much."

I love the fact there is an optimum number of cats to enjoy in a pub, and that number of felines is 15. All the cats were born in the pub. One even popped out during the pub quiz. Imagine that!

> *"Question 19. A cat has just been born in a crisps box at the back of this very pub. Is the kitten a boy or a girl? For a bonus point, which flavour box was he or she born in?"*

Neko Bar Akanasu, in Tokyo, claims to be the first bar to cater for cats. That gives BYO (bring your own) a different meaning. The only problem would be opening hours, as cats do prefer to pop out in the wee small hours.

> *"Yeah Dave, I'm shattered. Been out all night drinking."*
> *"Who with? Johnny or Terry?"*
> *"No. Sprinkles and Mr Timpkins. They're cool cats. But it all kicked off outside the kebab shop, when they started fighting over a bird. It was sad really, as she was already dead."*

Cat cafes have long been popular in Japan, where many people are prevented from owning pets as they live in small apartments. One has just opened in London called Lady Dinah's Cat Emporium. It is situated in Shoreditch, in East London. Of course it is!

Pub Parrots

A couple of people suggested parrots. Arguably the most popular parrot in pub history was Polly, who frequented Ye Olde Cheshire Cheese, in Fleet Street, at the turn of the last century. Polly was a he, an African Grey, who incredibly lived until the ripe old age of 40. According to *The Angus Evening Telegraph*, Polly was known for:

> *'His knowledge of Scottish words, which he ejaculated continually.'*

Is that a heavily laden euphemism for blue language? Polly was also known for:

'His imitation of the popping of corks'

Again, is that a euphemism?

Sounds a bit like Bubba Smith from the *Police Academy* movies. Legend has it that Polly disappeared in 1905. All was lost, until a man got into an argument with a dirty old man shouting obscenities from the shadows and begging:

"Gimme a kiss darlin'."

The dirty pervert was of course Polly, and that man was a policeman.

Rodents

There used to be a chain of pubs called The Rat and Parrot, which shut down in 2011. Not one of them housed a rat or a parrot – well, according to the health inspectors anyway.

My friend Simon used to have a pet rat called Rachel. She was a regular in his student bar at Reading Uni and used to hide in his woolly jumper. I remember going to a pub in Bristol with them both. It was a rough area, so Simon thought it prudent that Rachel guard the car. She would certainly have given any potential car thief a scare.

We do welcome the occasional rodent in the public bar of The Anchor, as some farmers like to keep a ferret in their trouser pocket. Why? A bachelor's prerogative I suppose. On one occasion, a dog sniffed out a ferret. Frightened, the ferret flew down the farmer's trouser leg, shot across the floor, shimmied up a stool and onto the bar. My Dad caught it by the tail. Inverted and apoplectic with fear, the ferret weed into the pint glass below, and turned a beer into a bitter shandy. Unfortunately, it wasn't a pint of Fursty Ferret. This comical story made the press, appearing in the 'Mean Fields' column of the *Daily Telegraph*, thus missing the opportunity of a *Sun* pun. Shame, as it missed such classy headline gems as:

Oh No Ro-Don't
Ferret Rochet – Unwelcome Reception
Wee Are Not Amused

Animal Friendly

Finally, when doing some research into the Tan Hill Inn, in North Yorkshire, I found a section which pleased me, in the frequently asked questions part of their website. It read:

'Are dogs allowed in your pub?'
'Yes, we're animal-friendly. They're even allowed to
stay in allocated rooms! We have even had sheep
and ducks in our pub. We love animals.'

What a delightful sentiment.

CONCLUSION AND THE SUN ACROSS WATER

23

THIS BOOK set out to crystallise what makes the perfect pub. I have proposed, discussed and dissected every aspect, nook and cranny of what constitutes the perfect British boozer. George Orwell waxed lyrical on his pub ideal in 1946. Seventy years on, I can think of no better ending to this book than a lighthearted contemporary tribute to his classic essay. Without further ado, I give you…

The Sun Across Water

My favourite pub, the Sun Across Water, is in an über hot spot, but it is off the beaten track so idiots can't find it, even with Google Maps.

It is a co-operative, jointly owned by local residents, without any tie to a brewery. The landlords are a hospitable husband and wife team, who know everyone by name and what they drink. This pub is a community hub where you can relax, have fun, plot and plan.

The first thing to strike you upon entering is its warm, welcoming atmosphere. Whether you pitch up with friends or saunter in on your own, you immediately feel at home and relaxed. This pub is not trying too hard to create a vibe, or follow fashions, trends and zeitgeists, it is a modern classic.

To begin with, its architecture and furniture is uncompromisingly finished (I don't mean Scandi style, I mean completed), unlike those hipster pubs with their semi-distressed walls, a neon Americana bar and a stag's head protruding and disturbing our taste. Taxi for taxidermy. Even if it has been previously nominated for the Turner Prize.

The bar is adorned by funky bar stools for barflies, with brass rails at the bar to hang your coat or bag on. Away from the bar there are straight-legged wooden Captain's chairs for all and a Chesterfield sofa to sink in, with the added bonus of hunks of loose change stuck down the side, to pep up the hungover and exhausted.

As W. H. Auden would say, "Stop all the clocks" – from hanging on the wall. A pub is a place to relax in idle contemplation without being reminded of the time-sensitive pressures of the outside world.

A roaring fire is heard to blaze and crackle in winter. In summer the only smoke is from the barbecue coals.

And so to drink. There is a good mix of real ale and other craft beer, both local and international, all reasonably priced. These are complemented by real and traditional ciders on tap. Seasonal ales are also on tap, such as light summer ales in June and pumpkin beers at Halloween. There is an actual Guinness fount, rather than nitro-pumped cans. It has fine and affordable house wine, fanning out to a wider selection for the more discerning. Behind the bar there is an arresting display of whisky and gin. The top shelf is aspirational, rather than terrifying, with high-end tequila and a sumptuous supply of port.

Surprisingly good, well-maintained toilet facilities are close at hand, with a plentiful supply of toilet roll and hot taps that provide actual hot water. This is not a nightclub. With that in mind, no toilet attendants will be loitering and peddling their perfumed wares, with infantile rhymes.

There is no background music, just the hubbub of keen conversation. Good sound-absorbing furniture prevents your conversation becoming too boomy, or echoing something embarrassing so that it hangs in the air like a clanger in a sitcom.

To this end, there is a separate sound-proof room in which to watch sport. It is called the dug-out and doubles up as a nuclear bomb shelter. This room also plays host to the pub quiz, a monthly comedy night, and the occasional live band. There is a pool table with enough room for your cue action. Across the room is table football, there is a quiet corner with a plentiful supply of board games, and a noisy nook for crashing Jenga.

One of the wonders of this pub is that there is never a queue to be served at the bar. The well-trained bar staff are friendly and attentive, without being over-familiar.

Unlike many pubs, there is a strong Wi-Fi signal throughout, and even a booster out the back. There are also phone-charging ports, subtly slotted into the furniture design. There are, however, no neon signs outside boasting of the boosted Wi-Fi, or that it is free.

The pub is known for its good comfort food, especially their Sunday roast dinner. The meat is succulent, whatever time you arrive, accompanied with seasonal, perfectly cooked vegetables and a huge home-made Yorkshire pud to mop up the onion and red wine gravy. The food is delicious and well appointed, without the pub becoming lost to the gastro world. Unusually, this pub has more than one vegetarian and vegan option on the menu, as less than two is not an option, but a necessity. Food is served on actual plates, not pine or slate.

You have to sample the irresistible pub snacks served in the bar. These include home-made Scotch eggs and sausage rolls, and a portion of perfectly cooked golden hand-cut chips, with a home-made spicy ketchup dip. On the crisp front, Brannigans Ham and Mustard is a must have. (Apologies to Americans for placing crisps and chips so close together, I know this flummoxes you guys.)

Where would we be without an assortment of good-quality nuts, from Brazil to cashew, spicy to roasted? My 1980s old-school vending machine is a quirky extra, for the nostalgia nut, with a penchant for Wham Bars, Space Invaders and Sherbet Dips.

Outside there is a beautiful south-facing, wasp-free garden, with plenty of shade from a weeping willow in summer, and outdoor burners for the colder months.

Unfortunately, this pub does not exist, it is a fantasy pub, and while some pubs contain some of these elements, I do not currently know of a particular pub which has all these attributes, but I do know a few which come close.

And if anyone knows of a dog-friendly pub, which has well-kept, reasonably priced ales, good service, a delicious roast and comfy chairs, please tweet me at @jamesdowdeswell #PubManifesto

Intriguingly, after all this pontification on the modern pub, I realise that my own views are not that far removed from Orwell's original ideal. Therein lies the man's transcendental genius. So, let's take Orwell's blueprint and tweak it into a modern classic. I still reserve the right for a '80s-type vending machine, a bouncy castle and a screening of a rare Aston Villa victory on the telly.

Bibliography and Further Reading

Great Books about Pubs

Jessica Boak & Ray Bailey, *20th Century Pub*, The Homewood Press, 2017

Pete Brown, *Man Walks into a Pub,* Macmillan, 2003

Pete Brown, *The Pub,* Jacqui Small, 2016

Paul Moody and Robin Turner, *The Search for the Perfect Pub*, Orion, 2011

Fine Writing on Food and Drink

Kingsley Amis, *Everyday Drinking*, Bloomsbury, 2008

Pete Brown, *Three Sheets to the Wind*, Pan, 2006

Oz Clark & James May, *Oz & James Drink to Britain*, Pavilion Books, 2009

Melissa Cole, *Let Me Tell You about Beer*, Pavilion Books, 2011

Jeff Evans, *CAMRA's Book of Beer Knowledge*, CAMRA Books, 2011

Michael Jackson, *Michael Jackson's Beer Companion*, Mitchell Beazley, 1993

Hugh Johnson and Jancis Robinson, *The World Atlas of Wine*, 7th edn, Mitchell Beazley, 2017

Tom Kerridge, *Tom Kerridge's Proper Pub Food*, Absolute Press, 2013

Historical Interest

Geoff Brandwood, *Britain's Best Real Heritage Pubs*, CAMRA Books, 2016

C. F. W. Dening, *Old Inns of Bristol*, John Wright & Sons, 1943; reprinted, The History Press, 2005

George Ford, *Thornbury Pubs*, Amberley Publishing, 2010

Arthur Taylor, *Played at the Pub: The Pub Games of Britain*, English Heritage, 2009

Good Pub Guides

CAMRA's Good Beer Guide 2019, CAMRA Books, 2018

Euan Ferguson, *Drink London: the 100 Best Bars and Pubs*, Frances Lincoln, 2014

Paul Moody and Robin Turner, *The Rough Pub Guide*, Orion, 2008

Acknowledgements

I would like to raise a glass and thank the following wonderful people:

My beautiful fiancée and best friend Leo, for all her love, generosity and support.

My Mum and Dad, for their inspiration, love and support, and raising me on real ale. My sister Talia, Mat Slade, Caroline and Derek Sweet for all their love, humour and encouragement.

All at CAMRA Books: particularly Simon Hall, for his infectious enthusiasm and drive; the discerning eye of my editor, Simon Tuite; Toby Langdon; Dale Tomlinson; Tony Lewis; and Katie Button.

Literary advice from Joe Melia and Oliver Rowe; contract advice from James Taylor and Katie Philips at Avalon.

COMEDIANS: Russell Howard, Jon Richardson, Dominic Frisby, Chris Gilbert, Vladimir McTavish, Al Cowlie, Mark Olver and Mike Tombs.

FORMATIVE VILLAGE DRINKERS: Simon Shaw, Steve Faulkner, Charles Offer, Jon Dyke, James Slade, Gavin Hogg and Philippa Moffat, who kindly suggested I write the book.

BRISTOL BOYS: Nick Cotter, Nige Fryer, Tim Greg, Ali Chambers, Chris Gillett and all The Pink Elephant Club.

SWANSEA UNI MOB: Andy Pank, 'Hippy' Jim Dancy, 'Yakka' Jim Anscombe, 'Aikido' Jim Barber, Lee Dainty and Andy 'Turmoil' Thomas.

BLACK BELT IN WINE CREW: Nick Cotter (again), Cassidy Dart MW, James Simpson MW, Chris Jones, Kevin Batchelor and Ross Brandon.

Finally, I hope this book inspires readers to many more fun-fuelled nights out, and that the British pub goes from strength to strength. Support your local pub. Cheers.

Books for Beer Lovers

CAMPAIGN FOR REAL ALE

CAMRA Books publishes a range of other titles on beer, pubs and brewing. Some of our latest titles are detailed below. You can buy our books – and a selection of beer-related titles from other publishers – from us direct, by visiting our online bookshop at **www.camra.org.uk/books** or calling **01727 867 201**. Discounts are available for CAMRA members.

Good Beer Guide 2019

Now in its 46th edition, the beer-lovers' bible is fully revised and updated each year to feature recommended pubs across the United Kingdom that serve the best real ale. The *Good Beer Guide* is completely independent, with listings based entirely on evaluation by CAMRA members. The unique breweries section lists every brewery – micro, regional and national – that produces real ale in the UK as well as mentioning their beers. Tasting notes for the beers, compiled by CAMRA-trained tasting teams, are also included. This is the complete book for beer lovers and for anyone wanting to experience the UK's finest pubs.

RRP **£15.99**   ISBN 978-1-85249-354-7

Essential Home Brewing

ANDY PARKER & GRAHAM WHEELER

Whether you're taking your first steps in home brewing, or you're a more experienced home brewer entering competitions or following a dream of brewing commercially, this book contains everything you need to know. From understanding and selecting your ingredients, through to equipment, the brewing process, and troubleshooting, this is a step-by-step guide to brewing your own great-tasting beer. Featuring 30 exciting recipes from world-leading, innovative craft breweries, with hints and tips on adapting the brews to make them your own.

RRP **£11.99**   ISBN 978-1-85249-351-6

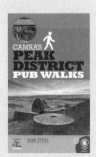

Peak District Pub Walks

BOB STEEL

Bob Steel's classic *Peak District Pub Walks* has been tempting people into the magnificent hills, dales and inns of the national park for over a decade. Now fully revised, this third edition introduces many completely new routes, revealing the wonderful diversity of the Peak landscape, and exploring of the area's abundant industrial heritage. An indispensable guide to the scenic highlights and some of the best pubs of the region for the outdoor enthusiast and real-ale lover alike.

RRP **£12.99**   ISBN 978-1-85249-353-0

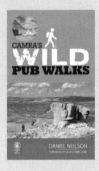

Wild Pub Walks

DANIEL NEILSON

The ideal book for hill walkers who enjoy long days out followed by a refreshing beer in a welcoming pub. Join author Daniel Nielson on 22 walks in beautiful remote or mountain landscapes, each with one or more great pubs at journey's end. The areas covered are: Peak District; Lake District; North York Moors and Yorkshire Dales National Parks; the Scottish Highlands and Islands; Scottish Borders; Snowdonia; Pembrokeshire and South Wales. The walks vary in the level of challenge, from long walks in lower-lying areas to Grade 1 scrambles.

RRP **£11.99**   ISBN 978-1-85249-340-0

Historic Coaching Inns of the Great North Road

ROGER PROTZ

The Great North Road is a UK icon, the Route 66 of Britain, but instead of gas stations and diners, we have magnificent coaching inns. Taking in the history of these buildings, as well as the literature that has celebrated them — from Charles Dickens through to J B Priestley — Roger Protz describes these coaching houses with an expert and discerning eye, producing not only a great pub guide but also a gazetteer of the history and culture that are draped along this iconic road.

RRP **£12.99**   ISBN 978-1-85249-339-4

Britain's Best Real Heritage Pubs (New Edition)

GEOFF BRANDWOOD

This definitive listing is the result of 25 years' research by CAMRA to discover pubs that are either unaltered in 70 years or have features of truly national historic importance. Fully revised, this latest edition boasts updated information and a new set of evocative illustrations. Among the 260 pubs, there are unspoilt country locals, Victorian drinking palaces and mighty roadhouses. The book has features describing how the pub developed, what's distinctive about pubs in different parts of the country, and how pubs provided take-out sales in the presupermarket era.

RRP **£9.99**   ISBN 978-1-85249-334-9

CAMRA's GOOD BEER GUIDE APP

CAMPAIGN FOR REAL ALE

4,500 Pubs from CAMRA's most recent *Good Beer Guide*

32,000 Pubs/Venues across the UK stocking Real Ale

1,750 UK Breweries & 7,500 Beers

Search for pub by Name, Location, Facilities

Over 30 Filters including
Dog Friendly, Food, Wi-Fi, Garden, Real Fire

Log your visits,
tag the beers tasted
and post messages
on an interactive
news feed.

Regular updates from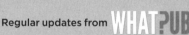

Unlock all functions for a subscription of
99p per month or £4.99 for 12 months

GET IT ON
Google Play

Download on the
App Store

Join the Campaign!

CAMRA, the Campaign for Real Ale, is an independent not-for-profit, volunteer-led consumer group. We promote good-quality real ale and pubs, as well as lobbying government to champion drinkers' rights and protect local pubs as centres of community life.

CAMRA has over 190,000 members from all ages and backgrounds, brought together by a common belief in the issues that CAMRA deals with and their love of good-quality British beer. From just £25 a year — that's less than a pint a month — you can join CAMRA and enjoy the following benefits†:

- Access to *What's Brewing* news and the award-winning *BEER* magazine, containing features and updates about beer, pubs and brewing.

- Free or reduced entry to over 200 national, regional and local beer festivals.

- Money off many CAMRA products and publications including the *Good Beer Guide*.

- Exclusive member benifits include 10% discount with Cottages.com, Cotswold Outdoor, Beer Hawk and many more.

- £20 worth of J D Wetherspoon™ real ale vouchers* (40 x 50 pence off a pint).

- Discounts in thousands of pubs across the UK through the CAMRA Real Ale Discount Scheme

- 15 months membership for the price of 12 for new members paying by Direct Debit**

For more details about member benefits please visit
www.camra.org.uk/benefits

If you feel passionately about your pint and about pubs, join us by visiting **www.camra.org.uk/join** or calling **01727 798 440**

For the latest campaigning news and to get involved in CAMRA's campaigns visit **www.camra.org.uk/campaigns**

†Membership prices and benefits are subject to change.
*Joint members receive £20 worth of J D Wetherspoon™ vouchers to share.
**15 months membership for the price of 12 is only available the first time a member pays by Direct Debit.